A FALSE NARRATIVE ENDANGERS THE HOMELAND

HEARING

BEFORE THE

COMMITTEE ON HOMELAND SECURITY
HOUSE OF REPRESENTATIVES

ONE HUNDRED THIRTEENTH CONGRESS

SECOND SESSION

JANUARY 15, 2014

Serial No. 113–47

Printed for the use of the Committee on Homeland Security

Available via the World Wide Web: http://www.gpo.gov/fdsys/

U.S. GOVERNMENT PRINTING OFFICE

87–941 PDF   WASHINGTON : 2014

For sale by the Superintendent of Documents, U.S. Government Printing Office
Internet: bookstore.gpo.gov   Phone: toll free (866) 512–1800; DC area (202) 512–1800
Fax: (202) 512–2250   Mail: Stop SSOP, Washington, DC 20402–0001

COMMITTEE ON HOMELAND SECURITY

MICHAEL T. MCCAUL, Texas, *Chairman*

LAMAR SMITH, Texas
PETER T. KING, New York
MIKE ROGERS, Alabama
PAUL C. BROUN, Georgia
CANDICE S. MILLER, Michigan, *Vice Chair*
PATRICK MEEHAN, Pennsylvania
JEFF DUNCAN, South Carolina
TOM MARINO, Pennsylvania
JASON CHAFFETZ, Utah
STEVEN M. PALAZZO, Mississippi
LOU BARLETTA, Pennsylvania
RICHARD HUDSON, North Carolina
STEVE DAINES, Montana
SUSAN W. BROOKS, Indiana
SCOTT PERRY, Pennsylvania
MARK SANFORD, South Carolina
VACANCY

BENNIE G. THOMPSON, Mississippi
LORETTA SANCHEZ, California
SHEILA JACKSON LEE, Texas
YVETTE D. CLARKE, New York
BRIAN HIGGINS, New York
CEDRIC L. RICHMOND, Louisiana
WILLIAM R. KEATING, Massachusetts
RON BARBER, Arizona
DONDALD M. PAYNE, JR., New Jersey
BETO O'ROURKE, Texas
TULSI GABBARD, Hawaii
FILEMON VELA, Texas
STEVEN A. HORSFORD, Nevada
ERIC SWALWELL, California

VACANCY, *Chief of Staff*
MICHAEL GEFFROY, *Deputy Chief of Staff/Chief Counsel*
MICHAEL S. TWINCHEK, *Chief Clerk*
I. LANIER AVANT, *Minority Staff Director*

(II)

CONTENTS

A FALSE NARRATIVE ENDANGERS THE HOMELAND

Wednesday, January 15, 2014

U.S. House of Representatives,
Committee on Homeland Security,
Washington, DC.

The committee met, pursuant to call, at 10:08 a.m., in Room 311, Cannon House Office Building, Hon. Michael T. McCaul [Chairman of the committee] presiding.

Present: Representatives McCaul, King, Broun, Miller, Meehan, Duncan, Marino, Barletta, Hudson, Brooks, Perry, Sanford, Thompson, Jackson Lee, Higgins, Richmond, Payne, O'Rourke, Horsford, and Swalwell.

Chairman MCCAUL. The Committee on Homeland Security will come to order. The committee is meeting today to examine the danger to the homeland from the threat of extremism. I now recognize myself for an opening statement.

Today the President's rhetoric on the threat of al-Qaeda and its franchises are in stark contrast to the reality we are witnessing in the Middle East and Northern Africa. Whether or not the downplaying of the spread of these Islamic extremist groups and the real threat they pose, which are metastasizing from the civil war in Syria, is to further a political agenda or simply to avoid the conflict altogether, I believe this false narrative greatly endangers our National security.

Protecting this Nation requires that we correctly identify the threats against it. It also requires that the United States lead on the world stage. I am increasingly concerned that we are doing very little of both. The administration has labeled the Fort Hood massacre in my home State "workplace violence," explained Benghazi away with a protest to a video as opposed to an al-Qaeda-driven attack, and removed words like "violent Islamist extremism" from their vernacular. With each attack, the administration appears to distance itself from who is behind it.

President Obama repeatedly tells us that al-Qaeda is on its heels and on the run. In May of last year, the President said that Osama bin Laden is dead and so are most of his top lieutenants, there have been no large-scale attacks on the United States, and our homeland is more secure. Killing bin Laden was an important accomplishment, but it has not put al-Qaeda on its heels or secured the homeland. In fact, Peter Bergen just recently wrote in an article last week that al-Qaeda appears to control more territory in the Arab world than it has done at any time in its history.

Foremost in the narrative is the administration's frequent use of the "core al-Qaeda concept." This is a false construct in my judgment and misleading for a number of reasons. Today there is no central al-Qaeda nucleus. References to a "core al-Qaeda" imply that its defeat would dismantle terrorist efforts around the world and eliminate the terrorist threat to the homeland. This is simply not the case. Over time the term "al-Qaeda" has come to symbolize an ideology of hate towards the West, with the goal of establishment of a Caliphate ruled by Sharia law and the pathway there through violent jihad. We are seeing it spread, play out in the Middle East, in Africa, and in the Caucasus. And although many terrorist groups subscribe to this ideology, we must understand that they are independent organizations planning and conducting operations without the oversight of an al-Qaeda central command.

The only core is the ideology itself, and the defeat of an ideology requires more than just drone strikes. The failure to recognize this truth prevents us from understanding the real threat from Islamic extremism and clouds our judgment in fighting against it. Ultimately, you cannot defeat an enemy you are unwilling to define.

The second part of the false narrative is our increasing willingness to abdicate our responsibility as a world leader. In the aftermath of World War II, President Truman said, "The peoples of the Earth face the future with grave uncertainty, composed almost equally of great hopes and great fears. In this time of doubt they look to the United States as never before for goodwill, strength, and wise leadership." Again today the people of the world face the future with grave uncertainty and they look to the United States for stable leadership.

We are witnessing a worldwide rebalancing as we have never seen before in modern history. This time, however, it is exacerbated by a Sunni-Shia sectarian conflict that has consumed the Middle East, caused great unrest across the region, and is forcing countries around the world to intercede. Yet our steadfast leadership is notably absent.

Terrorist groups are multiplying. They are spreading like wildfire, I would submit, like a spider web across Northern Africa. Foreign fighters are pouring in every day into Syria at an alarming rate, while Syria itself is being pulled apart by Saudi Arabia and Iran. Red lines are drawn and crossed, diminishing our world standing and forcing other countries to act where we have failed.

Our negotiations with Iran damaged our relationship with Saudi Arabia and Israel. American forces pulled out of Iraq, and al-Qaeda now has taken over Fallujah, once the symbol of the United States' commitment to stability in Iraq. We are pulling out of Afghanistan, where not so long ago the 9/11 masterminds plotted against the United States. In Egypt, we have been indecisive with our support while radical elements are growing.

Our lack of leadership has damaged our standing in the world and created a power vacuum being filled by terrorists who are prospering in our absence. President Kennedy told us, "Our strength, as well as our convictions, have imposed upon this Nation the role of leader in freedom's cause." I believe that statement is as true today as it was then. It is through our stable leadership and clearly identifying our enemies that we will secure the homeland and protect the American people.

I look forward to this distinguished panel's testimony and today's discussion. I want to thank all of the witnesses for being here today.

The Chairman now recognizes the Ranking Member, the gentleman from Mississippi, Mr. Thompson.

Mr. THOMPSON. Thank you, Mr. Chairman.

I also welcome our witnesses today.

Ms. Harman, good to see you. As you know, you were an original Member of this body when it was a select committee, without any jurisdiction. We still have a little bit around.

Chairman MCCAUL. We are working on that.

Mr. THOMPSON. Today's hearing seeks to examine whether U.S. policy to address unrest in the Middle East, the splintering of al-Qaeda, and the withdrawal of U.S. forces from Afghanistan and Iraq adversely affect homeland security in the United States. Such an examination must begin with an authoritative statement of this administration's policies and actions in each area.

However, because there is no witness from the administration for us to question about these policies, it is unclear how this hearing will aid this committee's understanding of these critical issues or help inform our oversight of the policies necessary to impact this Nation's homeland security.

It appears that this hearing begins with the assumption that to maintain safety and security within its borders this Nation must use its military to address every threat outside of its shores. Given such a perspective, the United States would be in a position of constantly engaging in military action abroad. After $1.5 trillion and 6,000 American lives lost, there are many in this country who want us to consider a viable exit strategy. There are also many people who believe that the safety of this Nation can be secured by means that are tailored to each circumstance based on a realistic assessment of the threat.

As we consider the threat, we must acknowledge our current posture. Most experts agree that the death of Osama bin Laden has substantially weakened al-Qaeda. Its capabilities to mount large-scale attacks have been reduced. However, al-Qaeda is more decentralized, more dependent on its affiliates, and has come to rely on its ability to radicalize and recruit distant recruits to carry out attacks. The lack of a clear organizational and leadership structure has severely diminished the group's ability to develop joint plans and wage large-scale attacks.

I am not advocating that America return to a pre-September 11 posture. I don't know anyone who would advocate such a position. However, we must plan based on the facts as they are, not the facts as they were. As a legislative body, we must ask serious questions about our homeland security policies and how our posture should be given the on-going dismantling of al-Qaeda. The Congressional Research Service has said that some of the questions we should ask involve the costs associated with continued U.S. military presence and the challenges of restoring the readiness of our forces. We must discuss a strategy that protects U.S. interests, as well as the integration of efforts across U.S. Government agencies in support of a broad U.S. political strategy.

As we consider our policies, we need to ask about the National security apparatus that has developed in this country. The revelations about the massive collection of information and the operation of the FISA courts have caused people to question how these activities have improved our homeland. I understand that the administration will announce its plans to revamp the NSA surveillance programs. I look forward to hearing about those plans. This committee needs to be part of the discussion about the effects that these metadata collection programs have on our homeland security.

Mr. Chairman, I agree that we need to take a serious look at how world events play into our homeland security policies. This Congress must be willing to legislate and make changes in the laws that affect the homeland security of this Nation. However, before we legislate, we need to be willing to discuss the law and the underlying policies with all the relevant parties, the Congress and the administration, in the room. I look forward to having that discussion. I also look forward to the administration being invited here to testify about how their overseas policies will affect our homeland security.

With that, Mr. Chairman, I yield back.

Chairman MCCAUL. I thank the Ranking Member.

Other Members are reminded that opening statements may be submitted for the record.

We are pleased here today to have four distinguished witnesses with us to discuss this important topic. First, we are delighted to have Senator Joseph Lieberman. He represented the State of Connecticut in the United States Senate from 1989 to 2013. In the months after September 11, Senator Lieberman led the fight to create the Department of Homeland Security, which led to the creation of this committee and the Senate Committee on Homeland Security, which he chaired until his retirement from Congress last year.

Next, we have our dear friend who served on this committee—she actually was sort of my boss, if you will. She was the Chairwoman of the Intelligence Subcommittee as I was Ranking Member—Congresswoman Jane Harman.

It is great to see you here today.

She represented California's 36th District in the U.S. House of Representatives from 1993 to 2011, served on multiple Congressional committees, boards, and commissions, including this committee and the House Permanent Select Committee on Intelligence and the House Committee on Armed Services. She is currently the president of the Woodrow Wilson International Center for Scholars and is a member of the Defense Policy Board and the Homeland Security Advisory Committee, among others.

It is great to see you.

Next, we are pleased to have a very distinguished witness, General Jack Keane, a retired four-star general who completed 37 years in public service in December 2003, culminating as acting chief of staff and vice chief of staff of the U.S. Army. He currently serves as chairman of the board of the Institute for the Study of

War and sits on the board of directors for MetLife and General Dynamics.

Thank you, sir, for being here.

Next is Dr. Seth Jones, the associate director of the International Security and Defense Policy Center at the RAND Corporation. He served as plans officer and adviser to the commanding general of the U.S. Special Forces in Afghanistan, as well as representative for commander of U.S. Special Operations Command to the assistant secretary of defense for special operations.

The witnesses' full written statements will be included in the record. The Chairman now recognizes Senator Lieberman for his testimony.

STATEMENT OF HON. JOSEPH I. LIEBERMAN, FORMER SENATOR FROM THE STATE OF CONNECTICUT

Mr. LIEBERMAN. Thank you, Chairman McCaul, Ranking Member Thompson. It is great to be back before you. Thank you for convening this hearing. Thanks for inviting me to testify. Thanks for putting me in the great company of the other witnesses at the table.

I think it is very important that you are holding this hearing, and let me briefly explain why. In the aftermath of the attacks of September 11, 2001, the overwhelming focus of our Government and of the American people was on the threat of terrorism. Twelve years later, this is no longer the case. Our loss of focus is in part a consequence of the success we have achieved, namely, that we have not had another catastrophic attack on our homeland since that terrible Tuesday morning in September 2001.

But pride in this achievement must be tempered by an awareness of some harsh realities. First, al-Qaeda and its affiliates remain a ruthless, determined, and adaptive adversary. Second, the underlying ideology that inspires and drives al-Qaeda to attack us and our allies, namely, the ideology of violent Islamist extremism, is neither defeated nor exhausted. It manifests itself not just in a resurgent al-Qaeda, but in terrorist organizations that are either unaffiliated with al-Qaeda or loosely affiliated with it but have exactly the same goals and capability to use violence against innocents.

For that reason, our safety as a Nation is ultimately inseparable from our ability to meet the fullness of the threat. Our security as a Nation also requires, as you have said, that we stay engaged in the world beyond our borders. That is the best way to prevent another terrorist attack against America like the one that occurred on 9/11.

Yet increasingly we hear voices on both sides of the political spectrum who say that the threat of terrorism is receding, that the end of this conflict is here or near, and therefore that we can withdraw from much of the rest of the world. That narrative, as the title of this hearing suggests, is false and really does endanger our homeland.

There is no question that the United States under President Bush and President Obama has inflicted severe damage to core al-Qaeda, the senior leadership that reconstituted itself in the mid-2000s in the tribal areas of northwestern Pakistan after they were driven by the courageous American military from neighboring Afghanistan after 9/11. But to borrow a phrase from General Petraeus, while the progress we have achieved against core al-Qaeda is real and significant, it is also fragile and reversible. For example, and this is a very timely example, core al-Qaeda in the tribal areas of Pakistan has been degraded by the persistent, targeted application of military force against those individuals and networks.

The precondition for those operations and the intelligence that enables them has been America's presence in Afghanistan. If the United States withdraws all our military forces from Afghanistan at the end of this year, the so-called "zero option," which some now advocate, you can be sure that al-Qaeda will regenerate on both sides of the Afghan-Pakistan border. If you doubt that, I urge you to look at what is now happening in western Iraq, where just a few years ago, during the U.S.-led surge, al-Qaeda was dealt an even more crippling blow than core al-Qaeda has suffered in Pakistan. Yet now it is al-Qaeda that is surging back in Iraq, hoisting its black flag over cities like Fallujah and Ramadi and murdering hundreds of innocent Iraqis just in the last year.

To me this leads to an important conclusion, which is that while space for core al-Qaeda in tribal Pakistan has been shrunk, thanks to persistent U.S. action and leadership, new territory where al-Qaeda affiliates can find sanctuary has grown significantly during the same period, particularly in the Middle East and North Africa and sub-Saharan Africa. Al-Qaeda and other violent Islamist extremist groups have long exploited Muslim-majority countries that have been weakened or fragmented by conflict and neglected by the international community, including the United States. They take advantage of these places to recruit, radicalize, and train the next generation of extremist foot soldiers. They use these places to plot and plan attacks, including against our homeland.

That is why al-Qaeda and its affiliates first went to Afghanistan in the 1990s, that is why they later turned to Yemen and Somalia in the 2000s, and that is why today they are fighting to build sanctuaries in Syria, Iraq, and Libya. There is now a clear, present, and increasing threat to America and our allies from those three countries, but administration policymakers have signified that any involvement, and I stress any involvement by the U.S. military there is for all intents and purposes off the table. That means that the United States will not be able to assist our local allies in combating the rise of al-Qaeda in these countries. It also means that we are failing to help deal with the underlying conditions that are making al-Qaeda's resurgence possible.

To put it as bluntly as I can, I do not today see a credible or coherent American strategy for these countries—Syria, Iraq, and Libya—that most threaten to emerge as al-Qaeda's newest and most dangerous footholds, places from which terrorist attacks against our homeland can and will originate.

This failure, it should be added, has consequences for our National security that extend beyond counterterrorism. Across the Middle East and beyond, the credibility of American leadership is being questioned as it has not been for a very long time. Among friends and enemies alike there are doubts about our staying power, questions about our reliability as an ally, and suspicions that at the end of the day America will hesitate to back up our promises and historic commitments with the use of force if necessary in a dangerous world. That is the reality, I believe, of how the United States is seen right now in too many places in the world.

Some in Washington look at what is happening in Syria, Iraq, and Libya and downplay their significance for our security and with it our need to get involved. Yes, al-Qaeda-affiliated groups are there, these skeptic say, but they are mostly focused on fighting other Muslims. The situation is confusing and chaotic, we are told, and after all, these Sunni-Shia conflicts have gone on forever and will go on forever. "It is someone else's civil war" is a familiar refrain we are hearing often again. That is, again, a very false and dangerous narrative.

But keep in mind that 20 years ago, during the 1990s, most people in Washington dismissed what was happening in Afghanistan as "someone else's civil war," and thus began the road to 9/11. I fear very much that 20 years from now, or less, someone else is going to be sitting here testifying before this committee saying much the same about pulling back from Syria, Libya, and Iraq today.

In brief, what do I think the United States should be doing now to protect our people against future 9/11 attacks? First, I don't advocate sending tens of thousands of troops to these countries. I don't believe it is within our power or our responsibility to solve every problem these countries face. These are the standard, and I think hollow, straw man arguments against what we can and should do. There is a lot we can and should do.

In Syria, we can and should much more aggressively provide militarily-relevant support to non-extremist rebel forces. In Iraq, we can and should make clear to the government that we are willing to support Iraqis against al-Qaeda with U.S. air power, as well as putting a small number of embedded advisers on the ground while using that increased assistance as leverage to encourage the Maliki government to politically reconcile, particularly with Sunnis. In Libya, we can put in place, and should, a large-scale, well-resourced U.S.-led effort to build up the new Libyan Army and security forces as quickly as possible.

In Afghanistan, we can choose not to squander the gains of the past decade and dishonor the brave Americans who risked and lost their lives there. Instead, we can keep a sufficient follow-on military presence to sustain the increasingly-capable Afghan National Security Forces in our shared fight against al-Qaeda and the Taliban. That will also safeguard, incidentally, the gains that have been made in human rights and human development more broadly, particularly among Afghan women, all of which will be erased if the Taliban returns.

Mr. Chairman, Ranking Member, none of these possible actions by the United States represent simple or quick solutions. There are no easy solutions to this threat. But there are smart, strong steps we can take that will put us in a better position to deal with the evolving threats we face here at home and that will ultimately make us safer as a country.

Mr. Chairman, I would just ask unanimous consent that the rest of my statement be entered into the record as if read. I thank you again.

Chairman McCAUL. Without objection, so ordered. Thank you, Senator, for your analysis.

[The prepared statement of Mr. Lieberman follows:]

PREPARED STATEMENT OF JOSEPH I. LIEBERMAN

JANUARY 15, 2014

Thank you, Chairman McCaul, Ranking Member Thompson, distinguished Members of this committee. I am grateful for the opportunity to appear before you to testify today.

Let me begin by commending you for holding this hearing. In the aftermath of the attacks of September 11, 2001, the overwhelming focus of our Government and of the American people was on the threat of terrorism. Twelve years later, that is no longer the case. Our loss of focus is in part a consequence of the success we have achieved—namely, the fact that we have not had another catastrophic attack on our homeland since that terrible Tuesday morning in September, 2001.

The absence of such an attack, however, is not because of an absence of terrorist plots or plans against us. Rather, it has been the consequence of vigilance, determination, courage, and creativity by National security professionals and National leaders across two administrations, as well as the close cooperation and help of America's allies and partners around the world. It is also due to a series of sweeping National security reforms and innovations enacted in the aftermath of 9/11 that have made our Nation safer.

Pride in this achievement, however, must be tempered by an awareness of several harsh realities. First, al-Qaeda and its affiliates remain a ruthless, determined, and adaptive adversary. Second, the underlying ideology that inspires and drives al-Qaeda to attack us and our allies—the ideology of violent Islamist extremism—is neither defeated nor exhausted. It manifests itself not just in al-Qaeda but in terrorist organizations that are either unaffiliated with al-Qaeda or loosely affiliated with it.

For that reason, our safety as a Nation is ultimately inseparable from our own ability to adapt to meet this changing threat. It also requires that we stay engaged in the world beyond our borders. That is the best way to prevent another terrorist attack against America like the one that occurred on 9/11.

Yet increasingly we hear voices—on both sides of the political spectrum—who say that the threat from terrorism is receding, the end of this conflict is here or near, and therefore that we can withdraw from much of the rest of the world.

This narrative is badly and dangerously mistaken.

There is no question, the United States—under President Bush and President Obama—has inflicted severe damage to "core" al-Qaeda, the senior leadership that reconstituted itself in the mid-2000s in the tribal areas of northwestern Pakistan, after being driven by the American military from neighboring Afghanistan after 9/11.

To borrow a phrase from General David Petraeus, while the progress we have achieved against core al-Qaeda is real and significant, it is also fragile and reversible.

What has degraded core al-Qaeda in the tribal areas of Pakistan has been the persistent, targeted application of military force against these individuals and networks. The precondition for these operations, and the intelligence that enables them, has been our presence in Afghanistan. If the United States withdraws all of our military forces from Afghanistan at the end of this year—the so-called "zero option," which some now advocate—you can be sure that al-Qaeda will regenerate, eventually on both sides of the Afghan-Pakistan border.

If you doubt this, I urge you to look at what is now happening in western Iraq, where just a few years ago, during the U.S.-led surge, al-Qaeda was dealt an even more crippling blow than core al-Qaeda has suffered in Pakistan. Yet now it is al-Qaeda that is surging back in Iraq, hoisting its black flag over cities like Fallujah and Ramadi, murdering hundreds of innocent Iraqis this year, with violence surging back to 2008 levels.

This leads to an important conclusion. While space for core al-Qaeda in tribal Pakistan has been shrunk thanks to persistent U.S. action in recent years, new territory where al-Qaeda affiliates can find sanctuary has grown significantly during this same period, in the Middle East, North Africa, and Sub-Saharan Africa.

Al-Qaeda and other Islamist extremist groups have long exploited Muslim-majority countries that have been weakened or fragmented by conflict, and neglected by the international community. They take advantage of these places to recruit, radicalize, and train the next generation of extremist foot soldiers. They use them to plot and plan attacks.

That is why al-Qaeda and its affiliates first went to Afghanistan in the 1990s. That is why they later turned to Yemen and Somalia in the 2000s. And it is why today they are fighting to build sanctuaries in Syria, Iraq, and Libya.

Several factors make the prospect of al-Qaeda sanctuaries in these three countries especially dangerous for the United States and our allies. The first is their respective locations. Syria and Iraq are in the heart of the Arab Middle East, bordering key American allies like Jordan, Saudi Arabia, Lebanon, Turkey, and Israel. Libya and Syria are Mediterranean countries—comparatively easy to reach by terrorist recruits from the West, in contrast to remote Afghanistan and Pakistan. And Libya is also adjacent to the vast Sahel, with its weak and poorly-governed states.

In the face of the clear, present, and increasing threat to America and our allies from these places, American policymakers have signaled that any involvement by the U.S. military is for all intents and purposes off the table. This means that the United States is not effectively able to assist our local allies in combating the rise of al-Qaeda in these countries. It also means that we are failing to help deal with the underlying conditions that are making al-Qaeda's resurgence possible.

Put very bluntly, I do not see a credible or coherent U.S. strategy right now for exactly those countries—Syria, Iraq, and Libya—that most threaten to emerge as al-Qaeda's newest and most dangerous footholds—places, from which terrorist attacks against our homeland can and will originate.

According to one estimate, there are now more foreign fighters in Syria than in Iraq and Afghanistan combined over the past 10 years.

This failure, it should be added, has consequences for our National security that extend far beyond counterterrorism. Across the Middle East and beyond, the credibility of American leadership is being questioned as it has not been for a very long time. Among friends and enemies alike, there are doubts about our staying power; questions about our reliability as an ally; and suspicions that, at the end of the day, we will hesitate to back up our promises and historic commitments with the use of force—if necessary.

This is the reality of how the United States is seen right now in too much of the rest of the world.

Some in Washington look at what is happening in Syria, Iraq, and Libya and downplay their significance for our security, and with it, our need to get involved. Yes, al Qaeda-affiliated groups are there, these skeptics say, but they are mostly focused on fighting other Muslims. The situation is confusing and chaotic, we are told, and these Sunni-Shia conflicts have gone on forever. It is "someone else's civil war" is a familiar refrain we are hearing often again.

But keep in mind that 20 years ago, during the 1990s, most people in Washington dismissed what was happening in Afghanistan as "someone else's civil war." And thus began the road to 9/11. I fear very much that 20 years from now or less, someone else will be sitting here, testifying before this committee, saying much the same about pulling back from Syria, Libya, and Iraq today.

What do I believe the United States can and should do now to protect our people against future 9/11 attacks? First, I do not advocate sending tens of thousands of troops to these countries. Nor do I believe it is within our power, or our responsibility, to solve every problem these countries face. These are hollow straw man arguments against what we can and should do.

And there is much we can and should be doing today that we are not. In Syria, we can much more aggressively and creatively provide militarily-relevant support to non-extremist rebel forces. In Iraq, we can make clear to the government that we are willing to support Iraqis against al-Qaeda with U.S. airpower, as well as putting a small number of embedded advisors on the ground, while using that increased assistance as leverage to encourage political reconciliation. In Libya, we can put in place a large-scale, well-resourced, U.S.-led effort to build up new Libyan army and security forces as quickly as possible—rather than the balkanized, poorly-resourced, decades-long effort now in place.

And in Afghanistan, we can choose not to squander the gains of the past decade and dishonor the brave Americans who lost or risked their lives there. Instead we can keep a sufficient follow-on military presence to sustain the increasingly capable and courageous Afghan National Security Forces in our shared fight against al-Qaeda and the Taliban, that will also safeguard the gains that have been made in human rights and human development more broadly, particularly among Afghan women, all of which will be erased if the Taliban returns.

None of these possible actions by the United States represent simple or quick solutions. There are no easy solutions to the problems here. But there are smart, measured steps we can take that will put us in a stronger position to deal with the evolving threats we face and that will ultimately make us safer as a country here at home.

It is worth noting that, in all of these countries, we have repeatedly seen that al-Qaeda and its extremist vision for society are rejected by the overwhelming majority of people living there. In Iraq, Syria, and Libya, we have seen popular, grassroots movements rise up against al-Qaeda and other extremist groups. The question is whether we provide these anti-extremist popular movements with the help and support they need to succeed, or leave them on their own to fail.

This is especially urgent in Syria right now. In just the past several days, there has been a grassroots uprising in the northern part of the country against the al-Qaeda affiliate in Syria, because al-Qaeda has alienated the local population with its brutality and violence. The question is, do we now come to the aid of these rebels who are in a two-front fight against al-Qaeda and Bashar al Assad—which is to say, against Iran—and who desperately need our help? If we fail to do so, and al-Qaeda defeats them, the consequences will be dire not only for Syria, but for our own National security.

Let me make one final point. The Obama administration has repeatedly narrowed the rhetorical scope of this conflict from what it criticized as an amorphous and open-ended "war on terrorism" to an armed conflict against a discrete and identifiable group: al-Qaeda and its affiliates. Our goal, the President has said, is to disrupt and ultimately dismantle the entity known as al-Qaeda and those affiliated with it.

There is an argument for this approach. After all, the enemy we are fighting is not "terrorism," which is simply a tactic. But an organization-centric approach to counterterrorism, as the Obama administration has advocated, is ultimately inadequate because al-Qaeda as an organization can be eviscerated, but it will regenerate as long as the ideology that inspires it survives. An organization-centric approach may also inadvertently cause us to miss the threat posed by groups that share al-Qaeda's ideology and ambitions to harm us, but that lack meaningful organizational ties to it. Indeed, it seems plausible that this is part of what happened in Benghazi in 2012.

The fact is, ultimate success in the struggle we are in depends not simply on the death of particular terrorist leaders or the destruction of a particular terrorist group, important though that is. Rather, it requires the discrediting of violent Islamist extremism as a worldview.

And let me underscore here, the enemy is violent Islamist extremism—a political ideology that seeks to justify totalitarian governance by perverting religion. The enemy, we can never stress enough, is not Islam itself.

Nor, I would add, our enemy is political Islam per se. In fact, there are political Islamists who are neither violent nor extremist, and who recognize al-Qaeda to be a mortal threat just as much if not more than we do. In Tunisia, for instance, we see an Islamist party that has proven thus far to be respectful of democracy and of political pluralism.

In fact, such Islamists—operating in a democratic framework—may ultimately prove to be the most powerful and effective force to delegitimize and destroy violent Islamist extremism. Conversely, repressive regimes in Muslim countries are likely in the long run to radicalize people and push them towards violent extremism. For this reason, the United States does have a core National interest in the political development of the Muslim world towards greater freedom.

Mr. Chairman, the progress we have made since 9/11 in securing our homeland is real. But we should not delude ourselves into thinking that this fight is anywhere near over. Perhaps the best description of where we find ourselves can be found in the familiar words of a great statesman of the last century, speaking of a very different struggle against another totalitarian foe.

In late 1942, after the first British victories in North Africa, Winston Churchill told the House of Commons: "Now this is not the end. It is not even the beginning of the end. But it is, perhaps, the end of the beginning."

So, too, perhaps it is for us now "the end of the beginning" of our war against violent Islamist extremism. If so, that should give us reason to hope—but also grounds to recognize much danger, difficulty, and hard work lies ahead.

Chairman MCCAUL. The Chairman now recognizes our former colleague, Congresswoman Jane Harman, for her testimony.

STATEMENT OF HON. JANE HARMAN, FORMER REPRESENTATIVE FROM THE STATE OF CALIFORNIA

Ms. HARMAN. Thank you, Mr. Chairman. Good morning to so many good friends. This feels like a homecoming. As you pointed out, I spent 8 years on this committee, 4 when it was a select committee and then 4 when we finally eked out a little jurisdiction to form a real committee. I worked with most of you, certainly all of you in the top row. As you pointed out, Chairman McCaul, you and I were partners on the Subcommittee on Intelligence. Mr. Thompson, when he chaired the committee and when he was the Ranking Member, and I traveled the world looking at garden spots where terror cells are growing.

I feel that the history of bipartisanship of this committee has set an example for this House, and I hope it will continue to set an example for this House—and, oh, by the way, that other body somewhere in the Capitol—because my little deathless phrase that I have been repeating for years is the terrorists won't check our party registrations before they blow us up. We need to focus on this. Sorting ourselves out by party is not helpful.

Now I am at the Wilson Center, a garden of nonpartisanship—I have to say that feels very good—but I continue to focus on these issues. As you pointed out, I am on the Defense Policy Board, the State Department's Foreign Policy Board, the DNI board, and recently joined the Homeland Security Board, where I will hopefully advise Jeh Johnson in his new role, and I care intensely about the policies here and getting them right.

So in true bipartisan fashion, let me start with something not in my testimony, but that is an endorsement of some of the things you said, Chairman McCaul, and some of the thing you said, Ranking Member Thompson, in your opening statements, because I think they are both true, as are many of the things my dear friend Joe Lieberman just said.

Chairman McCaul, you said that the terror threat is growing and some are not paying adequate attention to that. The terror threat has changed from the 9/11 days. The core al-Qaeda, as I think you said, and I know Senator Lieberman said, has been substantially destroyed by the efforts of two administrations, one a Republican and one a Democrat. I think most people would agree that President Obama not only continued the efforts of President Bush, but he increased those efforts against core al-Qaeda, and most of those high-value targets have been removed. So it is less of a force.

But the terror threat has morphed. It is now a loosely-affiliated horizontal threat. Many of those groups are called al-Qaeda, some are, some aren't, but they are opportunistic, and they come together like cancer cells when necessary. The new organization, ISIS, the Islamist State in Iraq and Syria, is called al-Qaeda. It really isn't technically al-Qaeda. It was the old Zarqawi organization, that Osama bin Laden disliked, Zarqawi in Iraq was then taken out. But his successors run this organization, and it has taken advantage of an unfortunate vacuum in Iraq because, unfortunately, President Maliki, I think, makes inadequate efforts in some of the Sunni parts of his country, but also in Syria for obvious reasons.

So the terror threat has changed. But Ranking Member Thompson is also correct that to defeat this threat we need more than kinetic force. Playing Whac-A-Mole, which we have done pretty well and which we should continue to do in some parts of the world using drones and other activities, will eliminate individuals, but it won't defeat the threat. We really in the end have to win the argument.

That is why a whole-of-Government approach is so important. That approach is embraced by our Defense Department, oh, by the way, which has done some of this as a Defense Deferment, by our State Department, by public-private partnerships, by NGOs, and by many both in this body and around the world. We need, in addition to applying these strategies, to project an American narrative, and I think all of us agree on that, that explains what we are doing, why we are doing it, and persuades some kid in the boonies of Yemen not to strap on a suicide vest but rather to hopefully join a productive economy in his country, go to a school that doesn't teach extremism in the guise of having people memorize the Koran but teaches reasonable subjects in a truly dispassionate way. We have to help build those schools, by the way, and we have to make sure that girls get to go to them.

So I have a long statement here, but I want to now turn my focus, because I remember the 5-minute rule and I am about to exceed it, as did my buddy here, on two things that I think are the more immediate threats to the homeland, and they relate to terror, obviously, but I don't want us to lose sight as we are thinking about foreign terror organizations.

One of them is home-grown terror, something this committee has focused on extensively. Since 9/11, there have been almost 400 home-grown terrorists indicted on terror-related charges or killed before they could be indicted in this country. Lone wolves are a big part of this problem. This committee has studied—I know this because I was involved in it—how people who have radical beliefs, which are protected under our Constitution, then transition to wanting to be engaged in violent acts which are not protected. We passed legislation a couple of times, which unfortunately died in the Senate. But it is a huge issue, and we have to look at it in our country. Then we have to look at these disaffected Americans being recruited for attacks abroad by al-Shabaab, by groups in Syria, et cetera, all of which has been recently in the press.

But the other issue that is a huge imminent problem, and you and I were just talking about this, Mr. Chairman, is cyber terror. It is absolutely imperative that Congress pull together to pass legislation that gives our Government the tools to work with private industry, which is a huge partner in this, on solving this problem. Congress has been, alas, extremely partisan; there have been all kinds of problems why bills haven't passed. I know that Senator Lieberman and my dear friend Senator Collins had a bill in the Senate that they couldn't move. You just told me that there may be some chance of moving a bill here. I hope so, Godspeed, because we are way behind the curve in understanding, responding to, adapting to, and preventing cyber intrusions, especially in the private sector. Sadly, the leaks by Edward Snowden have given some of our tool kit to bad guys, our technical tool kit, and I think this is pernicious.

So in conclusion, the threats today are different. They are on a smaller scale, but they are very serious and we have to keep focused on it. We need a narrative and a whole-of-Government approach as much as or more than we need a kinetic approach, in my view. But endless partisanship is a huge obstacle to progress, and I urge this committee, in true Homeland Security Committee fashion, to pull together and do the right things about cyber terror, home-grown terror, and helping us make the wise decisions about a U.S. international role. Thank you, Mr. Chairman.

[The prepared statement of Ms. Harman follows:]

PREPARED STATEMENT OF JANE HARMAN

JANUARY 15, 2014

I've always said that terrorists won't stop to check our party registration before they blow us up. One of the hallmarks of my relationship with Chairman Michael McCaul was that we worked closely together to solve problems—we didn't let politics get in the way.

I'd like to make three basic points:

1. I watched closely for many years as al-Qaeda and associated terror groups changed. While the U.S. Government does not do a perfect job explaining the evolution, we are addressing new threats and in my own view making progress. A promising development is the indigenous push-back against the Islamic State of Iraq and Syria—or ISIS—in Syria. This is reminiscent of the Arab Awakening in Anbar, and might unify the Syrian opposition.

The problem with the U.S. narrative is not that we are underplaying the terror threat. We are inadequately explaining our agenda to people in the United States—and in the region. If we leave a vacuum, the bad guys fill it with their narrative.

2. Secretary John Kerry's efforts to negotiate peace in the Middle East and a nuclear deal with Iran are heroic and if successful will have a major impact on stability and security in the region. They will also "reset" how the United States is viewed.

3. Since 9/11, there have been almost 400 home-grown terrorists indicted on terror-related charges or killed before they could be indicted. The biggest threats to the U.S. homeland are home-grown, lone-wolf terror attacks and cyber-terror attacks.

   a. Lone wolves

- Radicalization is an individualized process and the vulnerable come from varied backgrounds. Recent reports that Syrian extremist groups are recruiting for U.S. attacks are extremely concerning. (See my *LA Times* op-ed dated January 6, 2014).
- Reverse recruitment is also happening, like al-Shabaab in Minnesota.

   b. Cyber terror

- We are way behind the curve in understanding, responding to, adapting to, and preventing cyber intrusions—especially in the private sector. We're just starting to protect better our physical computer systems. But we've barely touched security for mobile devices.
- Snowden leaks have compromised a lot of our technical ability. Some, like former Department of Homeland Security Assistant Secretary for Policy Stewart Baker, suggest that there are many countries that may have used the leaks to bolster their own capabilities. That means we lose the competitive edge.
- Most terror groups or lone wolves don't have advanced technical capability yet. But they learned quickly how to use the internet to radicalize, recruit, and fundraise; why wouldn't they learn how to launch attacks that way?
- It's not hard to buy exploits and find someone with the expertise to deploy them.
- So we have an opportunity now to harden our critical infrastructure. The President's Executive Order is a good start. But legislation is essential to compel industry to share threat data—not personal information about individuals—with the Department of Homeland Security and provide appropriate immunity when it does.

- H.R. 624, the Cyber Intelligence Sharing and Protection Act, (Rep. Mike Rogers) has passed the House. H.R. 756, the Cybersecurity Enhancement Act, (Rep. Mike McCaul) has passed the House. The Senate approach is different and progress is urgently needed.
- Spillover from the Snowden leaks has meant that businesses are even more reluctant to cooperate. We need more brain cells on this problem because it is the key to preventing a catastrophic attack.

So, what to do? Just as we've layered security across ports and transportation systems, we need to do the same in the cyber world. The SAFE Ports Act, a product of the House Homeland Security Committee (Lungren/Harman) in 2006, could be a model—leaving the more controversial pieces for stand-alone legislation.

CONCLUSION

1. Threats today are different and on a smaller scale. Al-Qaeda in the Arabian Peninsula describes this shift in its English-language on-line magazine *Inspire* as a "strategy of a thousand cuts." And they aren't expensive: "Operation Hemorrhage"—AQAP's printer-cartridge bombing attempt—cost less than $5,000.
2. We need a narrative and whole-of-Government approach more than kinetics.
3. But partisanship is a huge obstacle to progress.

Chairman MCCAUL. Thank you, Jane Harman. It is great to see you again.

Let me just say that today actually Congressman Pat Meehan and Yvette Clarke will be marking up our cybersecurity bill at the subcommittee level. I have enjoyed a good relationship with the Ranking Member, as you said, in the spirit of bipartisanship on this committee. I believe it will be passed, hopefully unanimously, just as the border security bill was passed unanimously out of this committee. I think when it comes to National security, as you say, they don't check our party affiliation, and we should be working together when it comes to National security. So thank you for that comment.

Next, the Chairman now recognizes General Keane for his testimony.

STATEMENT OF GENERAL JOHN M. KEANE, (RET. U.S. ARMY), CHAIRMAN OF THE BOARD, INSTITUTE FOR THE STUDY OF WAR

General KEANE. Good morning, Mr. Chairman, Ranking Minority, and distinguished Members of the committee. Thank you for inviting me to testify today on an important subject concerning the security of American people. I am honored to share this panel with three distinguished colleagues, particularly two friends, Senator Joe Lieberman and Congresswoman Jane Harman. Let me just say that they are both great American patriots, and I want to thank them publicly for their many years of devoted and selfless service to this great country.

You have asked to us consider the President's speech in May at the National Defense University as a basis for our commentary on the security of the United States and the American people. It is true that bin Laden is dead, there have been no major attacks on the homeland, and fewer troops are in harm's way. But it is not true that our alliances are stronger. Indeed, they are weaker because our allies are fundamentally questioning the will of the United States. Many allies believe the United States will not be there for them in a time of peril, and sadly some recent polling are indicating that the United States' standing in the world is at its lowest since prior to World War II.

How could this happen? Is this because of the protracted wars in Iraq and Afghanistan? Is it the U.S. backing of Israel and our inability to resolve the Israeli-Palestinian dispute? Absolutely not, in my judgment. It is because of American leadership. When American leadership is strong in the world, the world is a safer place. When American leadership is inconsistent, indecisive, and we are willing to permit others to lead who do not have the capacity, or when we are paralyzed by the fear of adverse consequence, then American leadership is weak and the world is a more dangerous place. As such, our adversaries are emboldened, they become more aggressive, they take more risk. The results are more death, more casualties, and the security of the American people is threatened. Tragically, this is where we are today.

Despite our success in denying sanctuary and driving the al-Qaeda from Afghanistan to Pakistan, defeating the al-Qaeda in Iraq, while also killing Osama bin Laden and many al-Qaeda leaders, the harsh reality is that radical Islam, the al-Qaeda and its affiliates, represent an ambitious political movement with a committed ideology. It is on the rise, and the evidence is overwhelming.

The al-Qaeda are quickly taking control of western Iraq, while they have seized control of northern Syria. The border is nonexistent, and today there is a bona fide sanctuary from which operations can be conducted against our allies in the region, specifically Jordan. The radical Islamists were not the catalysts for the revolutionary change that swept over the Middle East 3-plus years ago, but they see geopolitical change as opportunity to gain influence, and as such control territory and people. This is happening in Syria, Libya, Yemen, Tunisia, and Mali, while al-Qaeda affiliates are exerting pressure in Somalia and Kenya.

Because of the failure, in my view, of American leadership, the term "radical Islam" or "Islam extremism" is not mentioned in U.S. policy, which is quite astounding. Furthermore, 12 years after 9/11 we still have no comprehensive strategy to defeat radical Islam or al-Qaeda. We do not even have a military strategy. We use drones to kill al-Qaeda leadership in Pakistan and Yemen, as we should, but that is not a military strategy, it is a tactic and an instrument of war. It has limitations also because leaders are replaced quickly in an ideological movement and the mission goes on.

Contrast this current reality with our strategy and policies in the 20th Century when the United States was involved in another struggle, another ideological struggle, communism. We fashioned a grand strategy, we organized major alliances in Europe and Southeast Asia, in NATO and SEATO, to contain it by agreeing on a common political goal, as well as sharing intelligence, training, doctrine, equipment, and tactics. We encouraged some of our best universities to study the subject—whole departments grew up around the subject as a matter of fact—and think tanks like my colleague's, RAND and others, were initiated because of the challenge of communism.

After all, ideas in an ideological struggle truly matter. To understand our adversaries' ideas, their history of development, their weaknesses and strengths, and to challenge our own ideas against them is fundamental to defining and understanding our enemy. Today there is no such strategy. We have no formal alliances to partner politically, intellectually, and militarily against them. This is not about our troops fighting against the radicals world-wide, but assisting our allies so their troops can do it only when it is necessary.

I agree with Congresswoman Harman. This is a whole-of-Government approach, and it is largely nonkinetic. The radical Islamists understand us better than we do them. As such, they fear our ideas, democracy, and capitalism. The advancement of these ideas in the region is a major threat to radical Islamists because it makes it all the more difficult to bend the people's will and force surrender.

This is why the Arab Spring is such a threat to them. No one was demonstrating in the streets for radical Islam and jihad to achieve a better life. The people in the streets were looking at what the United States and the West has to help change their lives, political and social justice, economic opportunity. That is, democracy and capitalism. Therefore, the radicals are all in to influence the outcome that is so uncertain and unpredictable. On the contrary, ask any of our friends in the region about U.S. policy in the Middle East and the two most frequent descriptions are "disengagement" and "retreat."

No one can say with certainty, depending on open sources, that any one of these al-Qaeda hot spots that we have mentioned is a direct threat against the people of the United States. But this much we can say, that when we permit sanctuary and uninterrupted recruiting, training, planning, and equipping, as the al-Qaeda was able to do for almost 10 years prior to 9/11, then the risk to U.S. interests and the security of the American people is exponentially higher. After all, what makes this movement the most threatening we have ever faced is their stated and unequivocal desire to use WMD against the people of the United States.

Unchecked, radical Islam, an ambitious political movement, is in an ideological struggle with the United States and its allies that will dominate most of the 21st Century. We lost 3,000 Americans on our land and now almost 7,000 troops in foreign lands as we attempt to defeat it and our people and our way of life. We desperately need strong American leadership to define radical Islam for what it is, to fashion a comprehensive strategy, and to partner effectively with our allies to defeat it. We have a long way to go.

Thank you, and I look forward to your questions.

[The prepared statement of General Keane follows:]

PREPARED STATEMENT OF JOHN M. KEANE

JANUARY 15, 2014

Mr. Chairman, Ranking Minority, and distinguished Members of the committee, thank you for inviting me to testify today on such an important subject concerning the security of the American people. I am honored to share this panel with my distinguished colleagues and friends Senator Joe Lieberman and Congresswoman Jane Harman. They are both great American patriots and thank you so much for your many years of devoted and selfless service to the Nation.

You have asked us to consider the President's speech in May at NDU as a basis for our commentary on the security of the United States and the American people. It is true, that bin Laden is dead, there have been no major attacks on the homeland and fewer troops are in harm's way. But it is not true that our alliances are stronger, indeed, they are weaker because our allies are fundamentally questioning the "will" of the United States; many allies believe the United States will not be there for them in a time of peril and, sadly, U.S. standing in the world is at its lowest since prior to WWII. How could this happen? Is this because of the protracted wars in Iraq and Afghanistan, the U.S. backing of Israel and our inability to resolve the Israeli/Palestinian dispute? Absolutely not. This is because of American leadership. When American leadership is strong in the world, the world is a safer place. And when American leadership is inconsistent, indecisive, and we are willing to permit others to lead who do not have the capacity or when we are paralyzed by the fear of adverse consequence, then American leadership is weak and the world is a more dangerous place. As such, our adversaries are emboldened, they become more aggressive, they take more risks and the results are more death, more casualties, and the security of the American people is threatened. Tragically, this is where we are today.

It is undeniable that since 9/11 the United States has been at war with Radical Islam and, specifically, the al-Qaeda and its affiliates. This is a very ambitious political movement designed to control territory and people by first establishing a caliphate in Muslim lands and eventually seeking world domination. It is an ideology drawing extremist ideas from radical theologians and philosophers from the 14th Century on, yet grounded in Islam, which is its belief system. Jihad is the means to gain control using death and fear to force capitulation.

Despite our success in denying sanctuary and driving the al-Qaeda from Afghanistan to Pakistan, defeating the al-Qaeda in Iraq (which they openly admitted), while also killing UBL and many al-Qaeda leaders, the harsh reality is that Radical Islam and the al-Qaeda affiliates are on the rise and the evidence is overwhelming.

- After the strategic blunder of leaving no residual force in Iraq (and immunity for U.S. troops was a false issue) equally damaging, was distancing ourselves from a long-term strategic partnership between the United States and Iraq, leaving the al-Qaeda to have re-emerged and the level of violence today is as high as it was in 2008 and destined to get higher. The al-Qaeda are quickly taking control of western Iraq while they have seized control of northern Syria. The border between Syria and Iraq from a Radical Islamist perspective is non-existent and today there is a bona fide sanctuary from where operations can be conducted against our allies in the region, specifically, Jordan and other U.S. interests in the region.
- The radical Islamists were not the catalyst for the revolutionary change that swept over the Middle East 3-plus years ago, but they see geo-political change as an opportunity to gain influence and, as such, control territory and people. This is happening in Syria, Libya, Yemen, Tunisia, and Mali, while al-Qaeda affiliates are exerting pressure in Somalia and Kenya. In Egypt the Muslim Brotherhood won an election but failed their people when they attempted to impose an Islamist state on a secular nation.
- If we make the same mistakes in Afghanistan that we did in Iraq and pull the plug on support for the Afghans then the Taliban will truly threaten the regime and the al-Qaeda leadership will return to their most desirable sanctuary, the mountains of Afghanistan.

Because of the failure of American leadership the term Radical Islam or Islamic extremism is not mentioned in U.S. policy which is quite astounding. The great military strategists, Clausewitz and Sun Tzu, indicated that a major tenet in defeating an adversary is to define that enemy and equally important the nature and character of the kind of war they are waging. Furthermore, after 12 years of war, we have no comprehensive strategy to defeat Radical Islam or the al-Qaeda. We do not even have a military strategy other than counter insurgency in Iraq and Afghanistan. We use drones to kill al-Qaeda leadership in Pakistan and Yemen, but that is not a military strategy it is a tactic and an instrument of war. And it has limitations because leaders are replaced quickly in an ideological movement and the mission goes on. Contrast this current reality with our strategy and policies in the 20th Century when the United States was involved in another ideological struggle, Communism. We fashioned a grand strategy, we organized major alliances in Europe and Southeast Asia in NATO and SEATO to contain it by agreeing on a common political goal as well as sharing intelligence, training, doctrine, equipment, and tactics. We encouraged some of our best universities to study the subject and think tanks like Rand and others were initiated because of the challenge of Communism. After all, ideas in an ideological struggle truly matter—to understand our adversaries' ideas, their history of development, their weaknesses and strengths and to challenge our own ideas against them is fundamental to defining and understanding our enemy.

As stated, we have no strategy to defeat Radical Islam, we have no formal alliances to partner politically and militarily against them. This is not about our troops fighting against the radicals world-wide but assisting our allies so their troops can do it effectively, only, when necessary. I have been speaking on college campuses every year since 9/11 and I can assure you there are no departments at our great universities devoted to understanding this ideological struggle with Radical Islam, quite the contrary, if an academic pursues this line of scholarship it is often denigrated as not worthy of serious study.

The radical islamists understand us better than we do them. To illustrate, their initial strategic goal is to dominate and control Muslim lands. To accomplish this, their stated objective is to drive the United States out of this land, which is what 9/11 was about. But the reason is not the obvious one, U.S. military presence, which they do not fear and know they can harm but cannot defeat. Instead they do fear our ideas, democracy and capitalism. The advancement of these ideas in the region is a major threat to the Radical Islamists because it makes it all the more difficult to bend the people's will and force surrender. This is why the so called Arab Spring is such a threat to them. No one was demonstrating in the streets for Radical Islam and Jihad to help them achieve a better life. The drivers of the instability in this revolutionary change is political and social injustice and the lack of economic opportunity. The people in the streets are looking at what the United States and the West has to change their lives, democracy and capitalism. Therefore, the radicals are "all in" to influence the outcome that is so uncertain and unpredictable. On the contrary, ask any of our friends in the region about U.S. policy in the Middle East and the two most stated descriptions are "disengagement" and "retreat". The so-called "pivot" to the East with the emergence of China is camouflage for an unstated policy to disengage from the Middle East and, at all costs, to avoid the potential of another Middle East war. No one can say with certainty, depending on open sources, that any one of these al-Qaeda hot spots in the world is a direct threat against the people of the United States. But this much we can say, that when we permit sanctuary and uninterrupted recruiting, training, planning, and equipping as the al-Qaeda was able to do for almost 10 years prior to 9/11, then the risk to regional U.S. interests and the security of the American people is exponentially higher. After all, what makes this movement the most threatening we have ever faced is their stated objectives to use WMD against the people of the United States.

Unchecked, Radical Islam is an ideological struggle with the United States and its allies that will dominate most of the 21st Century. We lost 3,000 American citizens on our land and almost 7,000 troops in foreign lands as we attempt to defeat it and protect our people and our way of life.

We desperately need strong American leadership to define Radical Islam for what it is, to fashion a comprehensive strategy, and to partner effectively with our allies to defeat it. We have a long way to go.

Thank you and I look forward to your questions.

Chairman MCCAUL. Thank you, General.

I certainly agree, it is a war of ideology, that drone strikes have been effective, but I don't think alone they can kill an ideology and a movement. That is the great challenge we have today.

The Chairman now recognizes Dr. Jones for his testimony.

STATEMENT OF SETH G. JONES, ASSOCIATE DIRECTOR, INTERNATIONAL SECURITY AND DEFENSE POLICY CENTER, THE RAND CORPORATION

Mr. JONES. Thank you, Chairman McCaul, Ranking Member Thompson, Members of the committee.

There are obviously a range of perspectives on al-Qaeda and the threat to the United States from Islamic extremists. My own view and those noted both in my written testimony and oral testimony are informed by on-going work, my own work on this subject, including a forthcoming report on this, work that I am overseeing, and then my past service within U.S. Special Operations, and particularly visits recently, including to those same units overseas, especially Afghanistan, which I will come back to.

The argument that I will make here in my oral remarks will be several-fold. One is, while al-Qaeda and the broader movement has become decentralized, I think the data is important. What we have seen in running the numbers is an increase—an increase, a notable increase—in the number of what I will call Salafi-jihadist groups over the past several years, particularly since 2010, and especially in North Africa, in the Levant, Syria, Lebanon, and I am going to include the Sinai there.

Second, there has been an increase—again, an increase—in the number of attacks perpetrated by these organizations, and as part of that an increase in the casualties and fatalities that have come out of that. Now, while this trend is troubling in one sense, it is worth noting that not all of these groups are plotting attacks against the U.S. homeland and its interests overseas. So as I will come back to in a moment, I think it is worth highlighting which of these groups presents the most serious threat.

But I do want to note on the verge of the Sochi Olympics that we have multiple groups in the North Caucasus and in Central Asia that do present a threat to American citizens traveling to this area, to our athletes traveling to Sochi. So this threat obviously impacts us not just in our infrastructure overseas, like embassies, our homeland, but also major events like the Olympics.

I won't rehash the structure of this organization because my colleagues here have noted that, but I do want to highlight the fact that the biggest increase in what some have called the al-Qaeda movement has been in the organizations that aren't sworn affiliates, that is, they don't pledge allegiance to Ayman al-Zawahiri, the emir, but who have a very similar Salafi-jihadist world view, who would like to establish an Islamic emirate in areas they control. In particular, we have seen that increase in groups operating in North Africa and the Levant.

I will come back to the threat posed by those groups in a moment, but let me just shift to Afghanistan, where I visited not that long ago and where I have noted very serious concerns among U.S. military and intelligence units operating in these areas, that we have worked for a long time against groups operating in those areas. There is still a notable presence of those groups along a very porous border, both Afghanistan and Pakistan. We have tried for the last several years to kill or capture the emir of al-Qaeda in northeastern Afghanistan, Faruq al-Qatari, with limited success— no success, in fact. He has not been captured or killed.

I would just ask a rhetorical question that as we pull out our forces, close down our bases, and potentially even exit, will it be easier or harder to continue to target these individuals? I don't mean just with forces, but I mean collecting information, intelligence, on these individuals operating in this area. The answer is straightforward: It will be much more difficult.

I would say also that we have a number of groups that have plotted attacks against the U.S. homeland, this includes al-Qaeda, the Tehrik-e Taliban Pakistan, this area, the Times Square bombers, U.S. forces and U.S. Government installations in the region, and U.S. citizens, to include other groups, like Lashkar-e-Taiba, the Mumbai attacks, and the Haqqani Network.

Let me come just back briefly to this then what do these groups, what threat do they pose to the homeland? Again, in my view in looking at this problem set, the ones that pose the most significant threat at the moment to the homeland continue to be the group operating in Yemen, al-Qaeda in the Arabian Peninsula, and the inspired networks, like the Tsarnaev brothers that perpetrated the Boston bombings. But I would note that this was not just a homegrown plot. Both of the brothers listened extensively to al-Qaeda leaders, including the now-deceased Anwar al-Awlaki. They specifically used al-Qaeda propaganda in their attacks in Boston, including from the *Inspire* magazine. So there was a connection, just happened to be on the internet to what we consider core al-Qaeda.

We have got threats to U.S. embassies overseas from groups like al-Shabaab targeting plots, from Ansar al-Sharia in Tunisia, which has planned attacks against U.S. diplomats and infrastructure. We have got Americans, a growing number that has gone to Syria, Europeans that have gone to Syria. So again I would highlight that there is a very serious threat to U.S. infrastructure, citizens overseas. This is not just about homeland and this is definitely not just about the core al-Qaeda.

Let me just say in closing that we need a proactive policy. In my view, we have been reactive. We have now returned advisers and trainers into Somalia but we are reluctant to do that in Iraq. Trainers have been very useful on multiple levels. I think we did a phenomenal job during the Cold War of combatting Soviet Marxist-Leninist ideology. I think we have been very slow to develop a policy along those lines.

Let me just end by saying, with the NSA debates we cannot lose our ability to monitor individuals that have linked up with websites that are radicalizing Americans like the Boston bombers. So whatever happens with this NSA discussion, we cannot lose our ability to monitor those websites. Thank you, Mr. Chairman.

[The prepared statement of Mr. Jones follows:]

PREPARED STATEMENT OF SETH G. JONES [1]

JANUARY 15, 2014

Chairman McCaul, Ranking Member Thompson, and Members of the committee, thank you for inviting me to testify at this hearing, "A False Narrative Endangers the Homeland."[2]

There are a range of perspectives today on the threat to the United States from Islamic extremists. Some argue that al-Qaeda—especially core al-Qaeda—has been severely weakened, and there is no longer a major threat to the United States.[3] Former CIA operations officer Marc Sageman concludes that "al-Qaeda is no longer seen as an existential threat to the West."[4] Some contend that the most acute threat to the United States comes from home-grown terrorists.[5] Others maintain that al-

---

[1] The opinions and conclusions expressed in this testimony are the author's alone and should not be interpreted as representing those of RAND or any of the sponsors of its research. This product is part of the RAND Corporation testimony series. RAND testimonies record testimony presented by RAND associates to Federal, State, or local legislative committees; Government-appointed commissions and panels; and private review and oversight bodies. The RAND Corporation is a non-profit research organization providing objective analysis and effective solutions that address the challenges facing the public and private sectors around the world. RAND's publications do not necessarily reflect the opinions of its research clients and sponsors.

[2] This testimony is available for free download at *http://www.rand.org/pubs/testimonies/CT403.html.*

[3] R. Clapper, *Worldwide Threat Assessment of the U.S. Intelligence Community* (Washington, DC: Office of the Director of National Intelligence, March 2013). Academic arguments include, for example, John Mueller and Mark G. Stewart, *Terror, Security, and Money: Balancing the Risks, Benefits, and Costs of Homeland Security* (New York: Oxford University Press, 2011).

[4] Marc Sageman, "The Stagnation of Research on Terrorism," *The Chronicle of Higher Education,* April 30, 2013. See the response to Sageman by John Horgan and Jessica Stern, "Terrorism Research Has Not Stagnated," *The Chronicle of Higher Education,* May 8, 2013.

[5] Sageman, "The Stagnation of Research on Terrorism"; Sageman, *Leaderless Jihad: Terror Networks in the Twenty-First Century* (Philadelphia: University of Pennsylvania Press, 2008).

Qaeda is resilient and remains a serious threat to the United States.[6] Finally, some claim that while the al-Qaeda organization established by Osama bin Laden is in decline, "al-Qaedism"—a decentralized amalgam of freelance extremist groups—is far from dead.[7]

Which of these arguments is right? This testimony argues that while the al-Qaeda movement has become increasingly decentralized, there has been an increase in the number of Salafi-jihadist groups and followers over the past several years, particularly in North Africa and the Levant. Examples include groups operating in such countries as Tunisia, Algeria, Mali, Libya, Egypt (including the Sinai), Lebanon, and Syria. There has also been an increase in the number of attacks perpetrated by al-Qaeda and other Salafi-jihadist groups. While this trend is troubling, only some of these groups are currently targeting the U.S. homeland and its interests overseas like U.S. embassies and its citizens—a particular worry on the verge of the 2014 Sochi Winter Olympics. The most concerning are al-Qaeda in the Arabian Peninsula and inspired individuals like the 2013 Boston Marathon bombers, though the growing number of Western fighters traveling to Syria to fight against the Assad government presents a medium-term threat. These developments should cause serious concern among U.S. policymakers and, more broadly, the American population.

The rest of this testimony is divided into four sections. The first examines the organizational structure and capabilities of al-Qaeda and other Salafi-jihadist groups. The second section explores reasons for the resurgence of Salafi-jihadists. The third outlines implications of the U.S. withdrawal from Afghanistan, an important component of this hearing. And the final section outlines threats to the U.S. homeland and U.S. interests overseas.

THE ORGANIZATION AND CAPABILITIES OF SALAFI-JIHADISTS

Al-Qaeda and the broader Salafi-jihadist movement have become more decentralized over time. The unfortunate tendency among some journalists and pundits to lump all Islamic terrorists as "al-Qaeda" has clouded this debate. Consequently, I will focus on al-Qaeda and other Salafi-jihadists. Used in this context, Salafi-jihadists refer to individuals and groups—including al-Qaeda—that meet two criteria. First, they emphasize the importance of returning to a "pure" Islam, that of the Salaf, the pious ancestors. Second, they believe that violent jihad is "fard 'ayn" (a personal religious duty).[8] Salafi-jihadists consider violent jihad a permanent and individual duty.[9] Many Salafists are opposed to armed jihad and advocate the da'wa or "call" to Islam through proselytizing and preaching Islam. But Salafi-jihadists like al-Qaeda leader Ayman al-Zawahiri support both Salafism and armed jihad.[10]

Today, this movement is increasingly decentralized among four tiers: (1) Core al-Qaeda in Pakistan, led by Ayman al-Zawahiri; (2) a half-dozen formal affiliates that have sworn allegiance to core al-Qaeda (located in Syria, Iraq, Somalia, Yemen, and North Africa); (3) a panoply of Salafi-jihadist groups that have not sworn allegiance to al-Qaeda, but are committed to establishing an extremist Islamic emirate; and (4) inspired individuals and networks.

1. Core al-Qaeda.—This tier includes the organization's leaders, most of whom are based in Pakistan. Al-Qaeda leaders refer to this broader area as Khurasan, a historical reference to the territory that included Persia, Central Asia, Afghanistan, and parts of northwestern Pakistan during the Umayyad and Abbasid caliphates.[11] Core al-Qaeda is led by Ayman al-Zawahiri, but there are still a range of Americans in core al-Qaeda (such as Adam Gadahn) and operatives that have lived in America (such as Adnan el Shukrijumah). Al-Qaeda's senior leadership retains some over-

---

[6] Bruce Hoffman, "Al Qaeda's Uncertain Future," *Studies in Conflict and Terrorism,* Vol. 36, 2013, pp. 635–653; Bruce Riedel, "Al Qaeda is Back," *The Daily Beast,* July 26, 2013.

[7] Andrew Liepman and Philip Mudd, "Al Qaeda is Down. Al Qaedism Isn't," *CNN,* January 6, 2014. Accessed on January 12, 2014 at *http://globalpublicsquare.blogs.cnn.com/2014/01/06/al-Qa'ida-is-down-al-qaedism-isnt/.*

[8] See, for example, bin Laden's fatwa published in the London newspaper "Al-Quds al-'Arabi" in February 1998, which noted that "to kill Americans is a personal duty for all Muslims." The text can be found at: *http://www.pbs.org/newshour/updates/military/jan-june98/fatwa_1998.html.*

[9] Gilles Kepel, *Muslim Extremism in Egypt: The Prophet and the Pharaoh,* translated by John Rothschild (Berkeley, CA: University of California Press, 1993); Olivier Roy, *Globalized Islam: The Search for a New Ummah* (New York: Columbia University Press, 2004), p. 41.

[10] On Salafi-jihadists, for example, Alain Grignard, "La littérature politique du GIA, des origines à Djamal Zitoun—Esquisse d'une analyse," in F. Dassetto, ed., *Facettes de l'Islam belge* (Louvain-la-Neuve: Academia-Bruylant, 2001). Also see Assaf Moghadam, "The Salafi-Jihad as a Religious Ideology," *CTC Sentinel,* Vol. 1, No. 3 (February 2008), pp. 14–16.

[11] See, for example, letter from Ayman al-Zawahiri to Abu Bakr al-Baghdadi and Abu Muhammad al-Jawlani, May 2013.

sight of the affiliates and, when necessary, may adjudicate disputes among affiliates or provide strategic guidance. But Zawahiri's challenges with the Islamic State of Iraq and al-Sham highlight core al-Qaeda's limitations in enforcing its judgments. Around July 2013, Zawahiri took an unprecedented step by appointing Nasir al-Wuhayshi, the emir of al-Qaeda in the Arabian Peninsula, as his deputy, elevating the importance of Yemen for core al-Qaeda.

2. Affiliated Groups.—The next tier includes affiliated groups that have become formal branches of al-Qaeda. What distinguishes "affiliates" from other types of Salafi-jihadist groups is the decision by their leaders to swear bay'at (allegiance) to al-Qaeda leaders in Pakistan. These organizations include Islamic State of Iraq and al-Sham (ISIS) based in Iraq, al-Qaeda in the Arabian Peninsula (AQAP) based in Yemen, al-Shabaab based in Somalia, al-Qaeda in the Islamic Maghreb (AQIM) based in Algeria and neighboring countries, and Jabhat al-Nusrah based in Syria. All of the groups became formal affiliates within the past decade: ISIS in 2004, initially as al-Qaeda in Iraq; AQIM in 2006; AQAP in 2009; al-Shabaab in 2012; and Jabhat al-Nusrah in 2013 after breaking away from ISIS.[12]

Figure 1 highlights the number of attacks by al-Qaeda core and affiliates since 1998. The data indicate a substantial rise in the number of attacks over time. Most of these attacks have occurred in "near enemy" countries and against local targets. A further breakdown of the data shows that violence levels are highest in Yemen (from AQAP), Somalia (from al-Shabaab), Iraq (from ISIS), and Syria (from ISIS and Jabhat al-Nusrah). These attacks include a mixture of suicide attacks, complex attacks using multiple individuals and cells, assassinations, and various types of improvised explosive devices against local Government targets and civilians.

FIGURE 1.—NUMBER OF ATTACKS BY AL-QAEDA AND AFFILIATES, 1998–2012 [13]

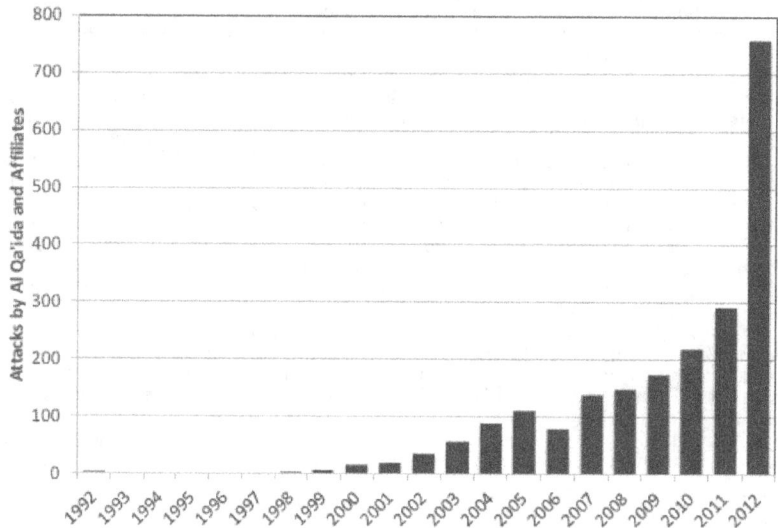

---

[12] These dates refer to the year in which the affiliate publicly announced that their emirs had sworn bay'at to al-Qaeda central leaders.

[13] Data are from the Global Terrorism Database at the University of Maryland's National Consortium for the Study of Terrorism and Responses to Terrorism (START). Accessed on January 12, 2014, at *www.start.umd.edu/gtd/*.

In Yemen, for example, AQAP retains a sanctuary in several governorates, including in southern Hadramawt, Shabwah, and Abyan along the Gulf of Aden—as well as around such cities as Rada' (in Al Bayda' governorate), Sana'a (Sana'a), Wadi Abidah (Ma'rib), and Yatamah (Al Jawf). The group has demonstrated an ability to mount large-scale, mass-casualty attacks across Yemen, especially in southern Yemen. AQAP has also benefited from limited Yemeni government operations. Since mid-2012, President Abd Rabbuh Mansur Hadi has avoided major ground offensives in favor of airstrikes and small-scale raids against al-Qaeda sanctuaries, perhaps to minimize government casualties. On September 30, 2013, for instance, al-Qaeda operatives overran the military's regional headquarters in Mukallah, Hadramawt governorate, killing at least 6. On September 20, al-Qaeda conducted a vehicle-borne improvised explosive device and small arms to attack military facilities in Shabwah Governorate, killing as many as 56 Yemeni security personnel. On December 5, al-Qaeda operatives launched a complex attack against the Yemeni Ministry of Defense complex in Sana'a, killing 40 Yemeni personnel and civilians, and wounding dozens more. They detonated a suicide vehicle bomb that breached a fence inside the compound, which allowed 6 or more militants to attack the military leadership hospital on the compound.[14] And on January 2, 2014, AQAP operatives were responsible for the assassination of a senior Yemeni security official in Aden. Most concerning, however, AQAP continues to plot attacks against the United States and American targets overseas.

3. Allied Groups.—Next are a series of allied Salafi-jihadist groups, whose leaders have not sworn bay'at to core al-Qaeda in Pakistan. This arrangement allows these Salafi-jihadist groups to remain independent and pursue their own goals, but to work with al-Qaeda for specific operations or training purposes when their interests converge. There are a substantial number of allied Salafi-jihadist groups across Asia, the Middle East, Africa, and the Caucasus. Perhaps most concerning, there has been an increase in the number, size, and activity of Salafi-jihadist groups in two areas: North Africa and the Levant. Examples include the Mohammad Jamal Network (Egypt), Ansar Bayt al-Maqdis (Egypt), Mujahideen Shura Council (Egypt), Ansar al-Sharia Libya (Libya), al-Murabitun (Algeria and other countries), Ansar al-Sharia Tunisia (Tunisia), Harakat Ansar al-Din (Mali), and Boko Haram (Nigeria).

4. Inspired Individuals and Networks.—The last tier includes those with no direct contact to al-Qaeda central, but who are inspired by the al-Qaeda cause and outraged by perceived oppression of Muslims in Afghanistan, Chechnya, Palestinian territory, and other countries. They tend to be motivated by a hatred of the West and its allied regimes in the Middle East. Without direct support, these networks tend to be amateurish, though they can occasionally be lethal. Tamerlan Tsarnaev, the ringleader of the 2013 Boston Marathon bombings, was motivated by the extremist preaching of now-deceased al-Qaeda leader Anwar al-Awlaki, among others. Tsarnaev and his brother also used al-Qaeda propaganda materials, including an article from *Inspire* magazine, to build the bombs.[15] But many others were rudimentary and their half-baked plots would have been difficult to execute.

WHY A RESURGENCE?

The rise in Salafi-jihadists groups has likely been caused by two factors. One is the growing weakness of governments across Africa and the Middle East, which has created an opportunity for Salafi-jihadist groups to secure a foothold. The logic is straightforward: Weak governments have difficulty establishing law and order, which permits militant groups and other sub-state actors to fill the vacuum.[16]

Governance, as used here, is defined as the set of institutions by which authority in a country is exercised.[17] It includes the ability to establish law and order, effec-

---

[14] Al-Qaeda in the Arabian Peninsula's media arm, al-Malahim, released a Twitter statement on @shomokhalislam regarding the December 5, 2013, and other attacks. See also HIS Jane's, Al Qa'ida in the Arabian Peninsula, December 2013, accessed Jane's World Insurgency and Terrorism database on December 19, 2013; "Al Qa'ida Claims Responsibility Over DOD Attack," *Yemen Post*, December 7, 2013.

[15] "Make a Bomb in the Kitchen of Your Mom," *Inspire*, Issue 1, Summer 1431 (2010), pp. 31–40.

[16] Ann Hironaka, *Neverending Wars: The International Community, Weak States, and the Perpetuation of Civil War* (Cambridge, Mass.: Harvard University Press, 2005); James D. Fearon and David D. Laitin, "Ethnicity, Insurgency, and Civil War," *American Political Science Review*, Vol. 97, No. 1 (February 2003), pp. 75–90. On the importance of building institutions, see Roland Paris, *At War's End: Building Peace After Civil Conflict* (New York: Cambridge University Press, 2004).

[17] World Bank, *Governance Matters 2006: Worldwide Governance Indicators* (Washington, DC: World Bank, 2006), p. 2.

tively manage resources, and implement sound policies. A large body of quantitative evidence suggests that weak and ineffective governance is critical to the onset of sub-state actors—including insurgent and terrorist groups. One study, for example, analyzed 161 cases over a 54-year period and found that financially, organizationally, and politically weak central governments render insurgencies more feasible and attractive due to weak local policing or inept counterinsurgency practices.[18] The reverse is also true: Strong governance decreases the probability of insurgency. In looking at 151 cases over a 54-year period, one study found that governance is critical to prevent insurgencies, arguing that success requires the "provision of temporary security, the building of new institutions capable of resolving future conflicts peaceably, and an economy capable of offering civilian employment to former soldiers and material progress to future citizens."[19] In addition, governmental capacity is a negative and significant predictor of civil war, and between 1816 and 1997 "effective bureaucratic and political systems reduced the rate of civil war activity."[20]

There are good reasons to believe that weak governance has contributed to the rise of Salafi-jihadist groups. Since 2010, a year before the Arab uprisings, there has been a significant weakening of governance across the Middle East and North Africa, according to World Bank data. Levels of political stability dropped by 17 percent from 2010 to 2012, government effectiveness by 10 percent, rule of law by 6 percent, and control of corruption by 6 percent across the Middle East and North Africa.[21] Of particular concern, governance deteriorated in numerous countries that saw a rise in Salafi-jihadist groups. Take rule of law, which measures the extent to which agents have confidence in and abide by the rules of society, as well as the quality of contract enforcement, property rights, the police, and the courts, as well as the likelihood of crime and violence. Between 2010 and 2012, rule of law dropped by 21 percent in Egypt, 31 percent in Libya, 25 percent in Mali, 20 percent in Niger, 17 percent in Nigeria, 61 percent in Syria, and 39 percent in Yemen. To make matters worse, most of the countries had low levels of rule of law even before this drop.[22] This decline appears to be, in part, a consequence of the uprisings.

A second factor is the spread of Salafi-jihadist militant networks within the Middle East and Africa. The logic is that operatives who have spent time training at al-Qaeda and other Salafi-jihadist camps or fighting in countries such as Iraq, Afghanistan, and Libya have moved to new countries in North Africa and the Levant and established Salafi-jihadist groups.

Individuals that spend time at training camps generally establish trusted social relationships.[23] Training camps provide a unique environment for terrorists to pray together, reinforcing their ideological views; share meals; train together in classrooms, at shooting ranges, and through physical conditioning; socialize with each other during breaks; and, after training is completed, sometimes fight together. Camps create and reinforce a shared religious identity and strategic culture dedicated to overthrowing infidel regimes.[24] For example, Umar Farouk Abdulmutallab, who attempted to blow up an airplane landing in Detroit on Christmas day 2009, attended an al-Qaeda training camp in the Shabwah region of Yemen. There were over 2 dozen fighters who dug trenches, crawled through barbed wire, and practiced tactical movements such as clearing buildings. The daily routine at the training camp consisted of rising early, praying, reading the Qur'an, completing warm-up drills, and conducting tactical training. After lunch, the students completed additional tactical training drills and stayed in tents at night.[25] The social interaction during daily routines experienced by individuals like Abdulmutallab creates a strong bond among operatives.

---

[18] Fearon and Laitin, "Ethnicity, Insurgency, and Civil War," pp. 75–76.

[19] Michael W. Doyle and Nicholas Sambanis, *Making War and Building Peace* (Princeton, NJ: Princeton University Press, 2006), p. 5.

[20] Hironaka, *Neverending Wars*, p. 45.

[21] World Bank, Worldwide Governance Indicators Data Set. Accessed December 16, 2013.

[22] World Bank, Worldwide Governance Indicators Data Set. Accessed December 16, 2013.

[23] Thomas Hegghammer, "The Recruiter's Dilemma: Signaling and Rebel Recruitment Tactics," *Journal of Peace Research*, Vol. 50, No. 1 (2012), pp. 3–16; Max Abrahms, "What Terrorists Really Want: Terrorist Motives and Counterterrorism Strategy," *International Security*, Vol. 32, No. 4 (Spring 2008), pp. 100–101.

[24] On identity and strategic culture see, for example, Alexander Wendt, *Social Theory of International Politics* (New York: Cambridge University Press, 1999); Peter J. Katzenstein, *The Culture of National Security: Norms and Identity in World Politics* (New York: Columbia University Press, 1996).

[25] See, for example, Umar Farouk Abdulmutallab Comments, Training Video of Abdulmutallab, Al Malahim Media Foundation (al-Qaeda in the Arabian Peninsula), Released in 2010.

The syllabi in many of these camps include theoretical and practical courses on weapons and explosives.[26] Individuals often study common religious texts in training camps, in addition to the Qu'ran and the hadiths.[27] Testimonies of former fighters suggest the camps foster a culture obsessed with weaponry.[28] Participants also engage in nasheeds, or battle hymns sung a capella during training and socializing. A similar component is poetry. Arab fighters in Afghanistan, Bosnia, Chechnya, and Iraq composed new poems and recited them in the camps. Veterans are often familiar with this material and share it during social gatherings. Another aspect of jihad culture is telling war stories from the time of the Prophet Muhammad and his immediate successors.[29] In short, the socialization process in camps, and later on the battlefield, develops and strengthens social bonds.

While there is limited data on foreign fighter flows, there is some evidence that individuals from al-Qaeda and other Salafi-jihadist camps and battle fronts have migrated to the Middle East and North Africa.[30] In Syria, for example, Jabhat al-Nusrah leaders, including Abu Mohammed al-Jawlani, were veterans of the Iraq war and members of al-Qaeda in Iraq. Mohktar Belmokhtar, the emir of Al-Murabitun, split off from al-Qaeda in the Islamic Maghreb in 2012 and had spent time in al-Qaeda training camps in Africa in the 1990s. In Egypt, Muhammad Jamal al-Kashif trained in Afghanistan in the late 1980s with al-Qaeda, where he learned to make bombs.[31] In Tunisia, Ansar al-Sharia's leader, Sayfallah Ben Hassine, spent considerable time at training camps in Afghanistan in the late 1990s and early 2000s, where he apparently met Osama bin Laden and Ayman al-Zawahiri.[32]

IMPLICATIONS OF THE U.S. WITHDRAWAL FROM AFGHANISTAN

The downsizing and potential exit of U.S. forces from Afghanistan—a focus of this hearing—could increase the terrorism problem from groups based in Pakistan, Afghanistan, and Central Asia. Al-Qaeda's global leadership is still located along the Afghanistan-Pakistan border, though it has been weakened by persistent U.S. strikes. A civil war or successful Taliban-led insurgency would likely allow al-Qaeda and other terrorist groups such as the Tehreek-e-Taliban Pakistan, Haqqani network, and Lashkar-e-Taiba to increase their presence in Afghanistan. Most of these groups have already expanded their presence in Afghanistan over the past several years and have attempted to conduct attacks either against the U.S. homeland (such as al-Qaeda and Tehreek-e-Taliban Pakistan), U.S. forces and U.S. Government installations in Afghanistan (such as the Taliban and Haqqani network), or U.S. citizens in the region (such as Lashkar-e-Taiba and al-Qaeda). Several Central Asian groups—such as the Islamic Movement of Uzbekistan (IMU), Islamic Jihad Union

[26] Rohan Gunaratna, "The Terrorist Training Camps of al Qaida," in James JF Forest, ed., *The Making of a Terrorist: Recruitment, Training and Root Causes* (Westport, CT: Praeger, 2006), pp. 172–193.

[27] See, for example, the study of Sayyid Imam Abd al-Aziz al-Sharif's works in al-Qaeda camps. Muhammad Hasan Khalil al-Hakim, "Jihad Revisions: Truths and Presuppositions," June 11, 2007, posted on a jihadist website.

[28] Omar Nasiri, *Inside the Jihad: My Life with Al Qaeda* (Cambridge, MA: Perseus, 2006). Also see the experiences of al-Qaeda operatives José Padilla and Najibullah Zazi. Declaration of Mr. Jeffrey N. Rapp, Director, Joint Intelligence Task Force for Combating Terrorism, submitted for the Court's consideration in the matter of *José Padilla* v. *Commander C.T. Hanft, USN, Commander, Consolidated Naval Brig,* Case Number 04–CV–2221–26AJ; *United States of America* v. *Najibullah Zazi,* United States District Court, Eastern District of New York, Docket No.: 09 CR 663 (S–1), Transcript of Criminal Cause for Pleading, February 22, 2010.

[29] Thomas Hegghammer, "The Recruiter's Dilemma: Signalling and Rebel Recruitment Tactics," *Journal of Peace Research,* Vol. 50, No. 1 (2012), pp. 3–16; Omar Nasiri, *Inside the Jihad: My Life with Al Qaeda* (Cambridge, MA: Perseus, 2006).

[30] On the transnational movement of terrorists see, for example, Thomas Hegghammer, "Should I Stay or Should I Go? Explaining Variation in Western Jihadists' Choice between Domestic and Foreign Fighting," *American Political Science Review,* Vol. 107, No. 1, February 2013, pp. 1–15; Hegghammer, "The Rise of Muslim Foreign Fighters: Islam and the Globalization of Jihad," *International Security,* Vol. 35, No. 3, 2011, pp. 53–94.

[31] United Nations, *Security Council Al-Qaida Sanctions Committee Adds Two Entries to Its Sanctions List* (New York: United Nations, October 2013). Available at: *http://www.un.org/ News/Press/docs/2013/sc11154.doc.htm.*

[32] U.S. Department of Defense, JTF–GTMO—CDR, MEMORANDUM FOR Commander, United States Southern Command, SUBJECT: Recommendation for Continued Detention Under DoD Control (CD) for Guantanamo Detainee, ISN US9TS–000510DP, September 15, 2008; U.S. Department of Defense, JTF–GTMO-CDR, MEMORANDUM FOR Commander, United States Southern Command, SUBJECT: Recommendation for Continued Detention Under DoD Control (CD) for Guantanamo Detainee, ISN US9TS–000502DP, June 22, 2007; Haim Malka and William Lawrence, *Jihadi-Salafism's Next Generation* (Washington, DC: Center for Strategic and International Studies, October 2013).

(IJU), and Jamaat Ansarullah (JA)—also could increase their presence in Afghanistan after the U.S. withdrawal.

Al-Qaeda leaders likely believe the U.S. drawdown will allow them more freedom of movement in provinces such as Kunar and Nuristan. Al-Qaeda's paramilitary commander and emir for northeastern Afghanistan, Faruq al-Qatari, is already attempting to expand al-Qaeda's footprint in the northeast.[33] Since al-Qaeda currently lacks the legitimacy and power to establish a sanctuary in Afghanistan and Pakistan on its own, it has attempted to leverage the capabilities of local militant networks like the Haqqani network. This symbiotic arrangement provides al-Qaeda some operational flexibility to access existing resources.

A burgeoning war could also increase regional instability as India, Pakistan, Iran, and Russia support a mix of Afghan central government forces, substate militias, and insurgent groups. Pakistan, in particular, would likely experience increasing violence and refugee flows if the war in Afghanistan spills over its border, as it did in the 1980s and 1990s. Growing conflict and radicalization in Pakistan, in turn, raises concerns about the security of its nuclear stockpile.[34] In short, a U.S. military departure from Afghanistan—if it were to happen—could foster a perception among some countries and organizations that the United States is not a reliable ally. Al-Qaeda and associated movements would likely view a withdrawal of U.S. military forces as their most important victory since the departure of Soviet forces from Afghanistan in 1989 and provide inspiration to core al-Qaeda, affiliated groups, allied groups, and inspired individuals and networks.

THE THREAT TO THE UNITED STATES

Not all Salafi-jihadist groups present a direct threat to the U.S. homeland. In the near term, al-Qaeda in the Arabian Peninsula likely presents the most immediate threat, along with inspired individuals and networks like the Tsarnaev brothers that perpetrated the April 2013 Boston Marathon bombings. The growth in social media and the terrorist use of chat rooms, Facebook, Twitter, YouTube, and other sites has facilitated radicalization inside the United States. While al-Qaeda leaders did not organize the Boston attacks, they played a key role by making available the propaganda material and bomb-making instructions utilized by the Tsarnaevs.

Other affiliates do not appear to pose an immediate threat to the U.S. homeland. Al-Qaeda in the Islamic Maghreb is focused on overthrowing regimes in North Africa, including Algeria. Al-Shabaab's objectives are largely parochial, and it has conducted attacks in Somalia and the region. But al-Shabaab possesses a competent external operations capability to strike targets outside of Somalia. The Westgate Mall attack was well-planned and well-executed, and involved sophisticated intelligence collection, surveillance, and reconnaissance of the target. These skills could be used for other types of attacks directly targeting the United States and its citizens. In addition, Americans from cities like Phoenix and Minneapolis have traveled to Somalia over the past several years to fight with al-Shabaab. Between 2007 and 2010, more than 40 Americans joined al-Shabaab, making the United States a primary exporter of Western fighters to the al-Qaeda-affiliated group.[35] And the Islamic State of Iraq and al-Sham, along with Jahbat al-Nusrah, are primarily interested in establishing Islamic emirates in Iraq, Syria, and the broader region.

Still, several Salafi-jihadist groups pose a threat to the United States overseas. Ansar al-Sharia in Tunisia, for instance, has planned attacks against U.S. diplomats and infrastructure in Tunis, including the U.S. embassy. Operatives from Ansar al-Sharia Libya, the Muhammad Jamal Network, and al-Qaeda in the Islamic Maghreb were involved in the 2012 attack that killed U.S. Ambassador Christopher Stevens. Several Salafi-jihadist groups pose a threat to the forthcoming Sochi Winter Olympics, including Imirat Kavkaz based out of the North Caucasus and the Islamic Movement of Uzbekistan.

Other groups, like Jabhat al-Nusrah, could be a long-term threat. Jabhat al-Nusrah's access to foreign fighters, external network in Europe and other areas, and bomb-making expertise suggest that it may already have the capability to plan and support attacks against the West. There appears to be a growing contingent of foreign fighters—perhaps several thousand—traveling to Syria to fight in the war. A substantial portion of these fighters are coming from the region, including Jordan, Saudi Arabia, and Iraq. Some have come from Chechnya. Others have apparently come from Afghanistan and Pakistan. But a significant number also appear to be

[33] Author interview with Western government officials, Afghanistan, September 2013.
[34] Author interviews with Pakistan officials, Washington, September 2013.
[35] Committee on Homeland Security, *Al-Shabaab: Recruitment and Radicalization Within the Muslim American Community and the Threat to the Homeland,* Majority Investigative Report (Washington, DC: U.S. House of Representatives, July 27, 2011), p. 2.

coming from the West, especially from Belgium, France, and Sweden. Extremists have traveled to Syria from other European countries. According to Spanish officials, for example, a network based in Spain and Morocco sent approximately 2 dozen fighters to Jabhat al-Nusrah over the past year. It is unclear how many of these fighters have returned to the West, but some have apparently returned to Germany, Denmark, Spain, and Norway among others. In October 2012, authorities in Kosovo arrested the extremist Shurki Aliu, who had traveled from Syria to Kosovo and was involved in recruiting and providing material to Syrian opposition groups. A small number of Americans—perhaps less than a dozen—have apparently traveled to Syria to fight with the Syrian opposition.[36]

It is currently unclear whether most of these fighters will remain in Syria over the long run, move to other war zones such as North Africa, or return to the West. And even if some return, it is uncertain whether they will become involved in terrorist plots, focus on recruiting and fundraising, or become disillusioned with terrorism. Still, foreign fighters have historically been agents of instability. They can affect the conflicts they join, as they did in post-2003 Iraq by promoting sectarian violence and indiscriminate tactics. Perhaps more important, foreign fighter mobilizations empower transnational terrorist groups such as al-Qaeda, because volunteering for war is the principal stepping-stone for individual involvement in more extreme forms of militancy. When Muslims in the West radicalize, they usually do not plot attacks in their home country right away, but travel to a war zone first. A majority of al-Qaeda operatives began their militant careers as war volunteers, and most transnational jihadi groups today are by-products of foreign fighter mobilizations.[37]

Based on these developments, U.S. policymakers should be concerned about the number, size, and activity of al-Qaeda and other Salafi-jihadist groups. Some of these groups pose a direct threat to the U.S. homeland, embassies, and citizens overseas, while others are currently targeting local regimes. Still, an effective U.S. strategy needs to begin with an honest assessment of the problem.

Chairman McCAUL. Thank you, Dr. Jones.

I agree that, you know, as al-Qaeda does spread—in a different form, Jane, you are absolutely right, they have evolved—but as it spreads, as Peter Bergen said, al-Qaeda has the largest presence now in the Arab world in history. So, too, does the threat to the homeland. That is my concern as Chairman of Homeland Security. I would also submit that the Boston, particularly Tamerlan, was not only inspired over the internet, but he did travel to Dagestan. He got through some of our flags, unfortunately. We will be releasing our report later this month on the Boston bombings, which I think will document some of these influences he had while he was over there.

General Keane, I would like to ask you my first question. In his new book, Secretary Gates wrote that under President Obama, the National security staff was, in his words, filled primarily by former Hill staffers, academics, and political operatives with little experience in managing large organizations, and that the National security staff became increasingly operational, resulting in micromanagement of military matters, a combination that has proven disastrous in the past. We have seen that in history.

This political heavy-handedness and the President's statements about al-Qaeda being on the run are concerning to me. Do you believe the administration is downplaying the threat of al-Qaeda to further their political goal of claiming victory in the Middle East?

General KEANE. Well, in my view, there is no doubt that they are downplaying it. You know, certainly championing the success of killing bin Laden and many of its leaders. But the fact of the mat-

---

[36] Author interview with government officials from Europe and the Middle East, April and May 2013.

[37] Thomas Hegghammer, "The Rise of Muslim Foreign Fighters: Islam and the Globalization of Jihad," *International Security,* Vol. 35, No. 3, Winter 2010/11, pp. 53–94.

ter is, as we have all testified here, it is clearly on the rise. It clearly is a threat to us here in the homeland and to our interests in the region.

Listen, this business of al-Qaeda becoming more decentralized is part of the plan. The al-Qaeda has always intended to take territory and gain control of people and to use affiliate groups in those countries as the start place, and then they bring foreign fighters to that scene. So what is being played out in front of us is part of their overall strategy.

Now, we have severed the command and control of that strategy to a large degree where they do not maintain operational control over this because of the pressure we have put on them, and that is a good thing.

Does that answer your question, Mr. Chairman? Okay.

Chairman McCAUL. Well, I think so. But again I think the al-Qaeda is on the run, this war on terror is over, I have personally experienced with the State Department and other agencies, traveling overseas, an attempt not to even use these words, to change the vernacular. Look, Jane, you know I am about as bipartisan as they come, but it concerns me that this language is taken out of the vernacular.

General KEANE. Well, I agree. Listen, I have had problems with the Bush administration in not educating the American people to what this movement is and keeping us posted on what our progress is against it. I challenged them for not having a comprehensive strategy to deal with this. It was taking sanctuary away in Afghanistan initially and then going after WMD in Iraq. But that is not a comprehensive strategy to defeat al-Qaeda, believe me.

This administration doesn't have it either. But it is even worse because it has got its head in the sand about it. One, it will not call it for what it is, it will not describe what it is, and it is downplaying the success the movement is having as it takes advantage of the revolutionary change that is sweeping through the Middle East.

Chairman McCAUL. I think that goes to the point, you can't defeat an enemy you cannot define. I think the head-in-the-sand analogy is correct. I think, frankly, they just want to say it is over and let's move on to something else. I don't know.

I do applaud the President with respect to bin Laden. I think that was a courageous effort, to go in with military forces and not just bomb the place, to prove to the world that bin Laden was killed. But I don't think that has solved the problem. It is not case closed anymore. This threat is growing throughout Northern Africa and the Middle East.

Senator Lieberman, just last week the House Armed Services Committee declassified testimony after months of hearing, and General Carter Ham, AFRICOM commander during the attack, testified. He said: To me it started to become pretty clear quickly that this was certainly a terrorist attack and not just something sporadic. I believe Leon Panetta was a part of this as well. The response, though, was not that this was an al-Qaeda attack, but blamed on some video and the protest over a video. What do you make of that?

Mr. LIEBERMAN. Well, a couple of things. The first is that it was obviously a terrorist attack by any generally-held definition of terrorism, which is the use of violence to achieve a political end or convey a political message. I mean, these are people who were attacking the U.S. consulate in Benghazi, and they obviously weren't there just to have a good time or because they didn't like that the consulate was there. They were there to make a statement against America, so it was classic terrorism.

Why there was hesitancy to do that at the beginning—frankly, even if it was in some way affected by the video, which I ended up concluding that if it was, it was only that the terrorist saw this as a moment of opportunity to strike—still it was terrorism. It is not as if, if you were affected by an awful grotesque anti-Muslim video and your response to that is to attack the U.S. consulate in Benghazi and burn it down and kill the U.S. ambassador, that is not terrorism.

The other thing I want to say, and this is based on an—unfortunately quick, because the session was ending—investigation that Senator Collins and I did of Benghazi in the last few months of 2012, one of the things we concluded—and I will say first for myself, I think some of the terrorists involved were either inspired or loosely connected to al-Qaeda, but a lot of them were indigenous and separate. Part of the problem, when you limit the enemy to al-Qaeda and affiliates and not to the broader category of violent Islamist extremists and terrorists is that you will miss part of the enemy, and part of our conclusion, Senator Collins and mine, was that we don't have adequate intelligence, at least we didn't at that point, on non-al-Qaeda clearly violent Islamist extremists.

Incidentally, in the last month, Ansar al-Sharia, Benghazi, was finally put on the foreign terrorist organization list, bringing about many things, including, I am sure, increased intelligence oversight of those groups.

Chairman MCCAUL. I agree with you. I think, you know, the distinction between core al-Qaeda, al-Qaeda, al-Qaeda affiliates, jihadists, I think they are all jihadists, and it is a movement that— that is a common thread, and the distinction without a difference, I think we need to be focused on the movement itself and not distinguish between all these different groups. They all stand for the same philosophy.

So, I would be remiss if I didn't give my colleague Jane Harman, who may not agree with me on everything, the last word.

Ms. HARMAN. Well, thank you, I appreciate that. I do think there was a terror attack in Benghazi, just to go over that point, and I do think we were underprepared. I recall that immediately afterwards Secretary—then-Secretary Hillary Clinton asked for a report and got 25 or 26 recommendations and implemented all of them. Hopefully, we will all learn the lessons of Benghazi, so that is point No. 1.

No. 2, though, I sit on these various boards in this administration, and they are bipartisan boards. I participate in discussions about these subjects because I am passionately interested in this stuff, as you all know, and I don't think we are being reactive. I think there are a lot of brain cells on this, both in these boards and in the administration in various departments.

I just came from 10 hours at the Defense Policy Board, and your old department, Jack, is all over this subject. Sure, maybe could be doing even better, but there was a discussion of South Asia that was pretty bone-chilling and a lot of people wanting to do a most effective job, but it does come back to something that General Keane said, which is whole-of-Government is a better approach to this than kinetics only.

I would just suggest, with respect, Mr. Chairman, that calling all of these different groups al-Qaeda emboldens al-Qaeda. That is something we don't want to do. If we can separate them and have strategies that take some of them out, which we do, not just with kinetics—I support the limited use of drones, but I also support other strategies—I think we will get farther.

Just, finally, you know, the world is extremely dangerous, but viewing this set of threats as the only threats I don't think is going to help us get to a place where the United States can project our power, all of our power, our smart power in the way that we need to. Looking at failing states and how we can support them is a high priority. Helping a transition to democratic with a small "d" regimes is another high priority, and building modern world structures. Some of the structures we deal with are pretty antiquated. That can project the whole of the world against, for example, the possibility of a nuclear action between India and Pakistan—those are Government decisions probably, although possibly could be loose-nuke-driven—it seems to me are also priority, so I just want to put this in a context.

Chairman MCCAUL. Let me close by saying, I think—and you will probably disagree with me on this. There has been a bit of a failure of leadership globally. I think our enemies view us as weaker, and they test us as a result of that more because they do view it that way, and our traditional allies, quite frankly, there is a lot of confusion over, where do we stand? Are we standing with them or not? Are we going to take out—are they going to be the next enemy of the United States we take out and create more instability that we have seen in the Middle East, particularly after this so-called Arab Spring?

With that, I now recognize the Ranking Member.

Mr. THOMPSON. Thank you, Mr. Chairman.

I don't think anyone on this committee, individually or all of us, want to do anything other than to keep Americans safe. I think how we approach keeping us safe is why we hold hearings like this, and we all have different approaches to keeping us safe. I think it is safe to assume that the collective of what I have heard today is really important. The difference of opinion is important. Somewhere between those differences is the security that we all are looking for. But a lot of us are faced, when we go to our districts, with an effort that has gone on a long time. People are becoming weary, not defeated but weary, and they say, why don't you do something to bring this to an end?

If we had a magic wand, we could do that. So, listening to some of our constituents who talk about the 6,000 people who died and the enormous cost so far, and I will go—because I have heard it—what would you suggest as a response to those constituents going forward as to what Members of Congress or the House and the Senate should do to bring that to an end?

I will start with you, Senator.

Mr. LIEBERMAN. Thanks, Congressman Thompson.

That is a really important question. I am very glad you asked it because that is the reality, and I know that is what you face and probably Members of both parties face when they go home.

So, here is the point at which—I mean, one first reaction I have, which won't really convince people, but it is an important one, and I will tell you that every time I went to a funeral of a soldier from Connecticut who was killed in Iraq or Afghanistan, I was amazed and moved by the families saying, please make sure that our son, daughter, husband, whatever, didn't die in vain. So, there is that element. I mean, if we just—we learned some lessons from Iraq and Afghanistan, but if we just walk away, we do risk saying to those families, whose family members gave their lives, because we ordered them to go there in our defense, that they did die in vain. I don't think we ever want that to happen.

The second thing I am going to go back to and in some sense is I want to make this personal about President Obama. Put it in this context. President Obama ran for office in 2008 and again in 2012 with one of the basic themes, in addition to all the change in dealing with domestic problems, was that, that he was going to get us out of the wars we were in and not get us into additional wars around the world. You know, fair enough, but sometimes, the world doesn't cooperate with a Presidential narrative, and I think that is where we are in the countries that I have talked about—Iraq, Afghanistan, Syria, Libya—which if we don't do something more than we are doing now, they are going to tip over.

So, I say this personally. I am not here just to criticize what the Obama administration has done. In some sense I am here to appeal to the Obama administration, which after all, the President is going to be our President for 3 more years, and a lot that could be good or bad for our security can happen.

I repeat: What is a lesson learned that is consistent with the message that the President, the policy that the President has adopted? We are not going to send tens of thousands of troops on the ground to any of these countries, but there is something in between that and just pulling out, and I think what we have all in different ways tried to argue today, both militarily and in other ways in terms of aid and support, we are—if we don't—and this is what I would say to the constituents—if we don't at least maintain a presence, we don't help the freedom fighters in Syria, the non-extremists anti-Assad people, if we don't build up the Lybian military to maintain order against the militias, if we don't make the kind of agreement and support the government in Iraq, then we are going to get attacked again. Same in—from Afghanistan, and then we are going to go back in there and have to spend even more and risk even more American lives.

It is not an easy argument, particularly not in tough economic times, but—so I think, bottom line, we learn from Iraq and Afghanistan. It is not going to be hundreds of thousands of troops, but if we just turn away, we are going to suffer, and therefore, we need your support, Mr. and Mrs. Constituent, to help us do that.

Ms. HARMAN. I can think—I can think of five things, some of which I have already mentioned, but I will tic them off.

One, honor the service of those who followed orders and went to Iraq and Afghanistan: 6,000 died, they leave behind families; many came home, tens of thousands grievously wounded; many came home in decent shape. Honor their service. Make sure we have in place a welcome mat that includes all the benefits they are entitled to but also, hopefully, efforts to build good jobs for them. The unemployment rate among returning vets is disproportionate to the unemployment rate of others.

Second, engage in a whole-of-Government approach to solve this problem. We have discussed that at length. I won't go into it again.

Third, continue the counterterrorism mission in not just the greater Middle East but around the world. The United States has interests in other places other than our own country, but we surely don't want training grounds to develop again in—pick a place—and we know that some are, and we need to be active there using all the tools that we have.

Fourth, continue our surveillance system, although I think some reforms are in order. The President will speak on Friday. I was quite impressed with the report that was presented to him. It is not clear exactly what he will adopt, but we need to have an effective system that can spot bad guys and prevent and disrupt plots against us.

Finally, enact cybersecurity legislation so that we are protected against what is a growing threat and could, in the end, be a more—many predict—a much more severe threat than some other form of terror threat against the homeland.

Mr. THOMPSON. General.

General KEANE. Yes. I would first say to them that never before in the history of the country have so few sacrificed so much for so many and have done it for so long. The fact of the matter is, the reason why it has been so long is because of the mistakes that we made, and be honest about it. The fact of the matter is, our strategy initially in Afghanistan, military strategy I am talking about here, and our military strategy in Iraq after we liberated Iraq was flawed, and that led to protracted wars, and we should have that honest discussion, you know, with the American people and also with your constituents.

Now, the fact of the matter is, if you know America's military, and I can say this with some knowledge, that we normally get off on the wrong foot, and we have throughout most of our history with some rare exceptions. But because we are reflections of the American people and American society, we are intellectually flexible and operationally adaptable, and we sort of get to the answer faster than other people would when we are at a much larger war than what we are dealing with here, and we did figure it out eventually in Iraq, and we have figured it out in Afghanistan as well, and the sacrifice is definitely worth it to protect the American people.

I mean, when you talk to the troops that we deployed in the 1990s, and we were all over the world doing things in Somalia, Haiti, Bosnia-Herzegovina, you name the place, there were problems, and we were there, not necessarily fighting to the degree that we have done post-9/11, but nonetheless, deployments and some fighting. From 9/11 on, and we have a 9/11 generation in the military, we have a 9/11 generation in the Central Intelligence Agency, the fact of the matter is when you talk to these troops, it is all about the American people. Before it was about helping others. This was about protecting the American people, and they get it. That is why they willingly go back and do four, five, six tours. We have generals that been away from their family for 8 out of 10 years. I mean, it is quite extraordinary the sacrifice that is willingly being made. Tell that story. It is extraordinary, because they are protecting the American people and our way of life, and they are willing do something that most of the American people cannot do, and that is, die for that, and that is really quite extraordinary.

So, I say be honest with them, and then, in terms of this troublesome area, I know intellectually we like to talk about we are pivoting to the east because of the emergence of China; does anybody in this room believe in the anywhere near term, we are going to war with China? Not that we shouldn't be vigilant about them. We can't be serious about that. The fact of the matter is, we have—we have huge problems in the Middle East that threaten the United States, and we have to stay engaged, Mr. Congressman. That is a word that we need to use. We partner with our allies in that region, and we support people who want to overthrow dictatorial regimes, like in Libya, like in Tunisia, like in Syria. Libya and Syria, they just want us to help them. They don't want our troops. In Iraq, where we did help them, we walked away, and look at the mess we have as a result. That should inform us of how dangerous this situation is and how important American commitment is to stay engaged. We have to do that if we are going to protect the American people.

Mr. THOMPSON. Dr. Jones.

Mr. JONES. I would say three things that are worth reminding constituents and all Americans that we talk to. One is, as much as we would like this war and the struggle to end, there are organizations committed to fighting Americans and conducting attacks overseas that will not end. They don't have a desire to end this, and the struggle on their part will continue. Therefore, the struggle continues. As much as we want to end it, the terrorists that we have talked about today are committed to continuing the struggle.

Second, I would say, as everybody here has noted, the days of large numbers of American forces targeting terrorists overseas, particularly conventional forces, are over. I think, as we have seen over the past several years, they have tended to radicalize populations rather than facilitate. So what that does leave us is, I would say, a third point, that there is a more modest approach. I think we have learned we are talking about smaller numbers of the forces but lethal ones overseas as well as civilians. We are talking about a smaller amounts of American dollars that are being spent. There is a need for direct action, some direct-action activity. We have stopped plots targeting the U.S. homeland from overseas with some of this action.

We also have an interest in building some local partnership capacity so that we don't have to do all of this, so that we don't have to do all the fighting and dying and that locals can do it. This is the direction we have moved on in several fronts, so I would say there has been a learning process. But let me just conclude by just, again, reminding constituents and Americans that from the al-Qaeda, the jihadist perspective, the war continues, and in that sense, we cannot retreat.

Mr. THOMPSON. Thank you.

Chairman MCCAUL. The Chairman now recognizes the Chairman Emeritus, Mr. Peter King from New York.

Mr. KING. Sounds like I am dead, anyway.

Chairman MCCAUL. No, you are not dead.

Mr. KING. Thank you, Mr. Chairman, and thank you for calling this hearing.

Let me thank all the witnesses for being here today.

I know Senator Lieberman and General Keane and Dr. Jones have all testified before.

Jane Harman, somehow, I think, she is still part of the committee. She was such an integral part in the formative years of this committee and the great work that you did. I also want, for the record, to point out that General Keane and I are the only two who do not have an accent.

I agree with virtually everything that was said here today, especially with the tone and the rational level of debate that we have had, and I do agree that there is a narrative which is hurting our country, and I think it comes from both—people in both parties, people in the media from all sides, really.

For instance, Congresswoman Harman, you mentioned, you know, the threat from domestic terrorism or home-grown terrorism. Well, there was no more effective force against, I believe, than the NYPD, and you have a personal interest in that since you have family members living in New York. Yet, if you read the *New York Times* for the last 3 years, it was editorial after editorial denouncing the NYPD, accusing them of profiling and going after innocent people, and yet, they did more to protect a major urban area than any other element in the country.

Dr. Jones, you mentioned the NSA and so did Congresswoman Harman, about the importance of it. We can have an intelligent debate about whether or not there should be certain reforms or what to be done and not done. I don't see that. In politics, we are talking about spying, about snooping. When you look at the, you know, the lettering during the TV shows, it is "NSA Scandal," despite the fact that the President's panel or no one has come up with even one abuse in all the years. So, rather than have an intelligent conversation, we go off on these, I think, too often, histrionics. You have people in both parties, including my own party, who talk about the U.S. being an imperial power, that somehow we want to be in wars. I think, as General Keane said, anyone who has been in the military knows, the last thing you want to do is be in a war, but that is the way the debate has been framed. There is virtually no talking about al-Qaeda.

I wish some of the people who rally against the NSA would spend equal time rallying against al-Qaeda. Sometimes you forget who the enemy is if you just listen to the media or listen to people in both parties. So I really want to thank you for coming here today, and really, I think, injecting a level of common sense that there is a real threat. In many ways, the threat is worse than it was before and more dangerous than it was before, and we have to deal with it in an intelligent way. Probably no one has done that as much or certainly not more than Joe Lieberman did during the time that he was in the Senate.

Congresswoman Harman, what you did in this committee.

General Keane, your service.

Dr. Jones, I am a great consumer of all the materials you put out, and thank you for the help you have given us.

Let me just talk about one particular area, and that is Syria, because there have been reports about how dozens of Americans, if not more, are going to Syria to take part in the fighting in Syria. They are siding with the al-Qaeda leading elements in Syria, and there is certainly the threat of them coming back here, you know, to this country, but even apart from that, when you are talking about western Iraq and Syria becoming a sanctuary for al-Qaeda, I would ask each of the four of you really, do you think it is too late for us to be providing aid to moderate elements in the Syrian resistance, or is it too much of a risk of that just enabling al-Qaeda itself or al-Qaeda affiliates, you know, to use it against us? So, I will just ask—and that will be my last question, ask each of the four of you, if you could respond, is what we should be doing in Syria, is it too late, and how effective can we be? Thank you very much.

Mr. LIEBERMAN. Thanks, Congressman King, thanks for your opening statement.

May I say personally, for a Chairman Emeritus, you are looking very good.

Mr. KING. Not as good as you, though.

Mr. LIEBERMAN. So, what was the question?

Oh, Syria. Okay. I got so embraced in how good you look, I forgot.

Okay. So, look, this is—this has been sort of a—this has been a story that has gotten more tragic as it is going on, and from the beginning, it seemed to me that we had—I went over there early on with Senator McCain. We met with the opposition figures there. As much as anybody can tell visiting, these were not extremists. These were genuine Syrian patriots, nationalists. They just were sick and tired of Assad's dictatorship, and frankly, just to go to both parts of what Jack Keane said earlier, democracy, capitalism, they felt that the Assad gang was stealing the Nation's wealth, and they didn't have an equal opportunity to build better lives for their family. We should have supported them from the beginning. It spun out of control.

But these people are not going to give up. They are still there. They are the moderate non-extremists sort of Syrian patriots, and since then, as you have said, Syria has become probably the front line of the al-Qaeda violent Islamist extremist war today because they are all pouring in, and they are linked now with what is happening in Iraq, but it is—the answer to your question, in my opinion, Chairman King, it is not too late.

If we sit back, frankly, it can only get worse. There are two bad results here. One is that Assad wins, which is a win for Iran incidentally, and the other is that the al-Qaeda groups win, so we still have a, what I would call, still, believe it or not, a pro-American element there, a group that we can work with. They are angry at us, they were disappointed with us, but they still need our help. You know, if it wasn't for the Saudis pouring money in there, they would have been—less moderate group would have been out already, so not too late. We have a lot on the line. If we don't act, Syria will become a base for future acts against the American homeland.

Ms. HARMAN. Congressman King, I have lots of positive things to say about the NYPD, in addition to the fact that they keep my kids and grandkids safe, and I think Ray Kelly's service was impressive. As you know, now, the new chief is Bill Bratton, who came from New York, but then he went to Los Angeles, where his skills improved as head of the LAPD, so now we send him back, the sleeker, better version of Bratton, and you will love him.

On Syria, it is a humanitarian catastrophe. This could be worse, in the end, than Rwanda and some of the egregious—certainly it is a humanitarian catastrophe of the 21st Century, as John Kerry just said. I think we should have acted years ago. Joe Lieberman and I agree, we didn't do it.

I do think there still is room to act, but we have to be quite careful about what we give to home. Wouldn't it be terrible if MANPADS surfaced and were used against Israelis by Hezbollah, or something of that nature? Because, again, of the way that these terror groups morph and unmorph and disperse, there is that risk, and the Intelligence Committees here and in the Senate looked at this and were pretty cool to giving them military weapons.

That said, however, I think the fact that Bashar has surrendered his chemical weapons should not be a permission slip for him to continue as head of the country, and I do think we need, and I think we are doing this through John Kerry, to focus on Geneva II, to getting the opposition there, including some of the more scary elements. Al-Nusra is part of the opposition that is not ISIS, and I think the goal has to be to provide humanitarian assistance, maybe, in some way, find a way to build humanitarian corridors so they can—that assistance can get to people who have been without food for—or any kind of sustenance for a long time, but then to shore up the opposition so that it can be the transition to a stable government without Bashar in it.

General KEANE. Yes, we certainly squandered a huge opportunity to be able to assist them. The fact of the matter is there was, even in the Central Intelligence Agency, when I was having discussions with General Petraeus, they were pushing back early on that the rebels were fragmented, unreliable, and just too much risk associated with harming them. But then, by the summer of 2012, actually, the Institute for the Study of War had some impact on the Central Intelligence Agency, and because we had some real evidence that the groups could be vetted properly, and the CIA did that, and as a result of that, the Central Intelligence Agency, then led by General Petraeus, gave briefings in Washington, obviously Classified at the time, that the rebels could be—could be armed and they could vet them. Secretary Clinton agreed with that, and that briefing went to the White House in the summer of 2012, and the President said no.

That, I think, was a strategic blunder on our part. As a result of that, the rebel organization, the Syrian Free Army, while still receiving weapons from Saudi Arabia, the fact of the matter is, they know, as a result of the last initiative dealing with chemical disarmament, they are probably not going to get help from the United States, and that group is less homogenous than what it was. A lot of the moderate Islamists that were associated with the Syrian Free Army have broken free of them because they don't think they are going to get the weapons.

The fact of the matter is, there is still opportunity there, and it is overstated about weapons falling into the al-Qaeda's hands. The Saudis have been giving these guys weapons now for 2-plus years, some of them are anti-aircraft weapons. To the best of my knowledge, and we stay pretty close on top of this, none of those weapons have found their way into the al-Qaeda, and the vetting that the CIA has done and the leaders they vetted are still there.

So, I do think there is opportunity, but we certainly did squander a huge opportunity a couple of years ago to truly make a difference.

Mr. JONES. This is a fundamental question, and you have, in multiple hearings, Congressman King, been on top of this issue, so thank you for continuing to bring it up.

In my view, it is not too late. We should have acted earlier. It is not too late. I would actually argue if we wait, if we continue waiting on this one, the trends are going to continue to get worse. So I think there is an incentive to do a couple of moderate things. I will not, I was in—in Europe, in Brussels, both to visit our partners, European partner agencies, intelligence agencies in December on the Syrian threat, and I have never seen the amounts of concern among the Europeans, number of Europeans that have gone to Syria to fight, well over a thousand, with, if they don't get on Watch Lists, will have Visa waiver access to the United States. Numbers up into the hundred, around a hundred or so Americans that have gone to either fight or otherwise participate in Syria.

The control of the territory that groups like Jabhat al-Nusra have had, have grown, and I think the more we wait, the bigger problem we have. What I would argue is—and there are two, I think, useful trends. One is the—the amount of support for the jihadist ideology in Syria is very small. As we have already seen recently with the push back against ISIL or ISIS, depending on which acronym you use, the al-Qaeda affiliate in the West, there has been active fighting against them because they have been involved in brutal killings, they have been involved in harsh reprimands against the local population, so I do think there is an opportunity, at the very least, to provide non-lethal communications equipment, information intelligence, and information could be actually quite useful for these organizations in their military and civilian strategies, blankets. I mean, there are a whole range of things, including to the refugees, that I think, again, that the longer we wait to act, the bigger this problem will continue to get.

Mr. KING. We thank all of them. I ask the Chairman if I could just have 10 seconds at the end. You know, in answer to the question of why these sacrifices were continuing, and every American death is absolutely tragic and profound, but keep in mind, on September 11, in less than 2 hours, we lost 3,000 people, and that is important to realize, that we are going to factor in again why these sacrifices are made, how vital they are, and what are the consequences if we ever again do let our guard down—3,000 in less than 2 hours.

I yield back. Thank you.

Chairman MCCAUL. I thank the Chairman. I just have one quick comment, and that is, with respect to Syria, I am very concerned this is a culmination of the Sunni-Shia conflict, and that it is becoming one of the largest training—terrorist training grounds now globally, and every day, jihadists are pouring into Syria.

I agree, General, that we squandered an opportunity 2 years ago when these forces were more moderate. I am concerned about the growing infiltration of the rebel forces by more extreme groups and the blow-back that that could present to the homeland.

With that, I want to say, given the time and the number of Members left, that the Chairman is going to stick very strictly now, I think, to the 5-minute rule.

The Chairman now recognizes the gentlelady from Texas, Ms. Sheila Jackson Lee.

Ms. JACKSON LEE. Let me thank the witnesses for their presentation today at a hearing that I hope, in its conclusion, will emphasize that there is no partisanship in the issue of domestic and National security.

I want to thank the witnesses for their thoughtful presentation, and in particular, to thank Senator Lieberman, Congresswoman Harman, and General Keane for their service to the Nation.

I think it is important to note that I hope in the course of the discussions about the issues of National and domestic security that we will quickly have before us the newly sworn-in Secretary of Homeland Security, which is a crucial issue, and that we will, like my Ranking Member has indicated, pursue the question of how you balance privacy and security with the question of the gathering of the mega data.

As a Member of the House Judiciary Committee, under the business section 215, that was not the intent of Congress, but I, as a Member of this committee, truly believe there should be a balance, and my questions will be along those lines of balancing, and I thank you very much for your presentation.

Let me also say that I am—I know Commissioner Kelly as well and certainly now Commissioner Bratton. Commissioner Kelly served in the Homeland Security department and respect his work. You can have security in New York, and frankly, we know the challenges it faces. Houston faces challenges because we are the epicenter of energy, but we can balance challenges with not having racial profiling. So I wanted to make sure I put that on the record because that is very important to us.

It is important also to note that President Bush had a series of Homeland Security security strategies that he offered in the 2000s. When President Obama came in, he integrated National security and domestic security, and I, frankly, think that was a very smart approach because National security is interwoven, meaning the security beyond the borders, making sure that this country defends itself from foreign enemies is the same, I think, of having domestic security, and that kind of structure is what I think that we should be looking at.

I have never conceded the point that al-Qaeda was dead, and I use the term rather than decentralizing, as franchising. Franchising was the shoe bomber. Franchising was the Christmas day bomber. Certainly in meetings that we have had, we know that al-Shabaab, although they have a pointed issue, they are after Kenya, but they are also reckless as it relates to Americans as well. So what goes on outside of our border impacts inside of our border, and frankly, this committee has worked hard, in particular, under HR 1417, a border security bill that has allowed us to work together.

Let me ask this question to everyone. In the Chairman's comments, he commented from Peter Bergen about the idea of an immediate threat at home. Peter states that al-Qaeda controls much of the Arab world, and therefore, what is its impact here?

My question is: Understanding that adjusting our approach to fighting terrorism is a broad perspective, can anyone identify areas of immediate need where the U.S. homeland is most vulnerable?

Let me start with General Keane, and if I can ask Senator Lieberman. My other question is: Is there any evidence that suggests that scaling back U.S. involvement and presence in countries such as Afghanistan and Iraq may reverse the efforts of the last decade to eliminate terrorist groups?

Might I also say, and I—your answers might also say that we wanted to pursue and stay in Iraq, but they had to protect our soldiers, and they refused to do it.

General Keane.

General KEANE. Yes. Well, certainly the engagement we have currently with senior al-Qaeda leadership in Pakistan is critical to American security. To continue to be successful at that, two things have to happen. One is we have to continue our involvement with the Pakistani military and assisting them to conduct counterinsurgency. In other words, unconventional operations against that force as well as the thing that they are most interested in is the Taliban that is threatening their regime. So our presence in Afghanistan, as previously stated by my colleagues here, is very important to us to be able to continue to have the intelligence we need and also the means to be able to execute operations against them. That is crucial.

Second, in my view, the developing situation in Syria and Iraq will become the largest al-Qaeda sanctuary, and it will threaten the region, to be sure, and we have to start now dealing with the harsh reality of that. The sooner we get on top of it in terms of intelligence, the better we are going to be with dealing with this reality.

This is what al-Qaeda wants. They will—they seize territory, gain control of people so that they can become predator in nature in that area, and also, they have never given up on their desire to cause more harm to the United States. So I think that is a major area.

I disagree with you, Congresswoman, on Iraq. The fact of the matter is, the immunity issue was not a serious issue. It was a false issue presented by Maliki as face-saving because the United

States envoy came in. After the military had recommended 24,000 soldiers to stay in Iraq, the President's envoy put 10,000 on the table. Maliki knew that was not a serious proposal. That eventually got down to nothing. The immunity issue got brought up at the end, and it was more face-saving for him inside of Iraq than anything else.

But the fact of the matter is, that is a significant strategic blunder not leaving forces there, much as we did post-World War II, not for security reasons but for influence, and we lost this influence over Maliki, and even further than that. It is more than the troops. We disengaged—disengaged geopolitically with Iraq and in terms of partnering with them, which they wanted very much so. They forced the strategic framework agreement on us. We wanted to have a status of forces discussion about troops, and they said no. Maliki said we are not doing that until we agree to have a strategic partnership that will last for 20 years. That was their idea. We walked away from that as well, and now we have this debacle on our hands.

So, that is the second-most—most critical area, I think, that we have to pay attention to, and without getting into the details of it, what has taken place in northern and northeastern Africa also is potentially threatening to us.

In principle, in my judgment, what you deal with, you cannot let sanctuaries take hold, and we should be using partnering with other countries to deal with those sanctuaries. I am not talking about bringing U.S. troops to bear. I am talking about, in some cases, in helping people with training assistance so they know how to deal with this problem, and we may actually help them with equipment and intelligence to deal with it, to be sure. But we cannot let these sanctuaries take hold and fester because they will be predator in nature on their neighbors and then eventually potentially dangerous to the American people.

Mr. LIEBERMAN. Just briefly, in answer to, Congresswoman, your very good question, which is, is there any evidence that our pulling out of countries creates a threat to our homeland—I am paraphrasing, but I think that is what you asked.

Well, I look back first at Afghanistan during the 1990s when, as I said earlier, the general feeling in this country was that was someone else's civil war when the Taliban took over and al-Qaeda nested there, and of course, that led right to the 9/11 attacks against us. Iraq today is another example of that. We pulled out for all the reasons that have been given here, and now al-Qaeda is back in, and they will—they will use that as a base against us.

I will summarize it this way. My reading of the last 15 years tells me that the reason that we have—and this—the reason that we have so diminished and degraded core al-Qaeda in the mountains between Pakistan and Afghanistan is not because of a whole-of-Government approach, because we used the U.S. military. I believe in a whole-of-Government approach, but that has to, in these cases, include the U.S. military because al-Qaeda is not a social organization. It has an ideological motivation to it, but it is a brutal military organization. We are only going to stop it by helping the heroes in each of these countries, who don't want al-Qaeda or the Taliban to control their lives and want to fight for something better. They need our help. They want our help, and if we give it to them, it will protect our homeland.

Ms. JACKSON LEE. Let me just say that I respect the testimony of the very fine witnesses. Many of us would disagree but agree that we have issues in both of those places, Iraq and Afghanistan, that I think we now need to collaboratively come together. I know the American people wanted out of the Iraq wars; they want out of Afghanistan. But they also want those countries to remain strong, to collaborate with them, to use resources, and as well they want us to have a strong National security policy that protects the homeland as well, and I think this is a very important hearing.

With that, Mr. Chairman, I thank you, and I yield back.

Chairman MCCAUL. Thank you.

The Chairman now recognizes the Chairman of the Cybersecurity Subcommittee, Mr. Meehan from Pennsylvania.

Mr. MEEHAN. I thank you, Mr. Chairman, and I want to thank again this very, very distinguished panel, not just for your presence here today but across the panel, your tremendous work on these issues on behalf of our Nation in so many different capacities.

Congresswoman Harman, it is indeed a pleasure to once again have the capacity to share a moment in this room with you. You will be pleased to know that—and I thank you for raising the issue of cybersecurity, because it—it remains a remarkable focus, and in the aftermath of the incident which just occurred with Target, and that is one kind of a cyber incident. Criminal enterprise is likely, wholly separate from the kind of state-sponsored cyber activity may take place.

So I want you to know we have made great progress, and we will be marking up this afternoon a cyber bill. But I am worried as well about the concerns that we may have in this Nation as we deal with the narrative in this moment that appropriately reflects in the aftermath of the NSA revelations and other kinds of things, we have got a better understanding, but there is a narrative that may be taking place, which is privacy versus security, and it is so easy for us to move so quickly away from attention to the security.

So I am going to ask if you would give me your sense of where we are in the form of the cyber preparation to deal with this issue of paying attention to protection of privacy but not surrendering in some kind of a knee-jerk effort our responsibility to protect Americans in so many different capacities.

Ms. HARMAN. Well, thank you, Congressman Meehan. It is very good to see you, too.

I—as I think about privacy and security, I often say they are not a zero-sum game. You didn't get more of one and less of the other. They are re-enforcing values, and things that we have worked on together in Congress, like the Intelligence Reform Law of 2004—Senator Lieberman, Senator Collins, Congressman Huckster, and I were the so-called Big Four on that one—not only find ways to re-organize our intelligence community so we leverage the strengths of all the agencies, but also to set up a privacy and civil liberties board, which was supposed to be stood up then and, unfortunately, hasn't—just finally was stood up last year. But at any rate, the point of that was to have, at the front end of policymaking, a group of people who worried about the privacy of Americans. We can do both. This needs to be a positive-sum game. It applies obviously to cybersecurity, and people are genuinely worried now that they see that there was a theft of I guess it is 70 million pieces of crucial information on individuals. That is a large number.

But they also need to be worried, it seems to me, about the purchase of exploits by bad guys, which are very inexpensive. These are back doors into our grids, our infrastructure in this country, and it is—so it is not just personal information. It is, you know, pick one, something very serious. It could be—generate, you know, a life-and-death problem for our communities.

So how to think about this? I think this committee has an opportunity, and I know you are doing it, to talk to the private sector, which controls most of the cyber capacity and persuade them to come on in. A cyber bill, Senator Lieberman knows this better than I do, has to grant immunity to those who come to play and has to respect the fact that personal information about companies is being shared and so on and so forth and make sure that again it is a win-win, and I think this is the climate to do it in.

I would just add on surveillance, because that has come up, too. Same issue. There is not a zero-sum game here. There should be tweaks, my view, to the laws that we have. I think the public debate is healthy, and the tweaks should assure an anxious public that their privacy is protected, but we should never compromise on the basic parts of the system that lead us to find bad guys before they attack us.

Mr. MEEHAN. Well, I thank you to for that, that answer. You will be pleased to see that I think we have made remarkable progress in the form of bringing together not just the private sector but our Governmental entities in the kind of a framework that would be effective, but the one place we haven't been able to touch, and you put your finger on it, is the kind of thing that will incentivize that sharing between the private and public sector which gives some kind of security really in the form of liability protection to those entities which are touched first. No better example than a Target who finds out, you know, weeks ahead of time that they are being impacted. We need to encourage that sharing in real time.

I thank you for your focus on this very, very important issue and look forward to working with the entire panel as we move through these issues in the future.

Thank you, Mr. Chairman. I yield back.

Chairman MCCAUL. Thank you. Let me just commend the gentleman for your leadership on this issue, your dedication to get not only the private-sector support of your legislation but also the privacy groups. It is not an easy task, and it is not—it is an uphill battle and you were able to accomplish that, and I just want to thank you for that.

The Chairman now recognizes the gentleman from New York, Mr. Higgins.

Mr. HIGGINS. Thank you very much, Mr. Chairman.

I just want to play a little bit more on this zero-sum game context. The one thing you know in a zero-sum game is that the sum will always be zero, but in game theory, there is also a variable-sum game where there can in fact be multiple winners, and there can only be multiple winners in a pluralistic society when the rights of minorities are protected.

There was a debate here last year about—or last couple of months about military intervention in Syria. We certainly did not support the Assad regime, the justification for authorizing the administration to use military force, albeit not troops on the ground, was that Assad had murdered, through chemical weapons, 100,000 people in Syria. Well, the rebel fighters were beheading people, and in that part of the world and in that conflict, I think the concern is not that you are supporting Assad, but as a minority, you are afraid that all non-Sunnis will be murdered.

Marwan Muasher just released a book called, "The Second Arab Awakening," and in it, he identifies the Middle East as being a pluralistic society, a pluralistic region of Sunni, Shia, Kurds, Christians, and a lot of tribes—and a lot of tribes. He also says that 500,000 American troops in Iraq and a trillion dollars couldn't implant a lasting pluralism or peace in Iraq, and therefore, no outsider can.

You know, what is going on in the Middle East today is it continued—the Chairman has said there was a culmination of Sunni-Shia conflict. It is really the continuation of it, and what is going on is Shia and Sunni are continuing to litigate a conflict that goes back to the Seventh Century as to who the rightful successor to the prophet Mohammed is. This is not about peace. This is not about democracy. This is about control, and so long as you don't have, as Fareed Zakaria would say, the inner stuffings, in his book, "The Future of Freedom," in a constitution that protects minority rights, you are always going to have these conflicts.

In Northern Ireland, George Mitchell was sent over there for 5 years, the last iteration was 22 months. He didn't think that peace was possible in Northern Ireland, and he says in his book "Making Peace" that the great intangible of solving conflict is exhaustion, not only at the negotiating table but also on the battlefield. The warring factions have to realize that their commitment to the fight, their commitment to the culture of violence has not produced any kind of lasting peace, and therefore, they need to move in a different direction.

So, what are the two sides in Northern Ireland, what were they required to do, the Catholics and the Protestants, the extremists? They were required to denounce violence and actually participate in destruction of their arms so that the culture of physical force to achieve political ends was over, but both sides had to give something in order to achieve that.

You know, you may say, you know, how can you compare Northern Ireland with the Middle East? Well, guess what, when George Mitchell was finished negotiating the Good Friday Accord, he was dispatched where? To the Middle East, because the conflict is very, very similar.

So, I just think that, you know, American Presidents certainly can do more to keep leaders in those countries from going to extremes, but there is only so much that we can do. Our American military has been extraordinary, extraordinary in tamping down violence in Iraq, tamping down violence in Afghanistan. To what end? We can't impose a political solution. We can only provide a context, a breathing space within which the warring factions can do that. I am afraid that in that part of the world, there are no good allies of the United States in that part of the world. Not Nouri al-Maliki in Iraq, not Karzai in Afghanistan. We have to bribe his brother to help promote a lasting peace in Afghanistan. We don't have good allies there.

What we can do I think is what we have already done, and I think we are limited. So, I am sorry I went on a little bit too long, but I am just interested in your thoughts about that.

Ms. HARMAN. Congressman Higgins, I don't know if I should be first, but I just very quickly would offer, too, first, I think we have some allies in the region, one of which Israel, which is a pluralist democracy and under threat. I strongly favor the peace process. I think it is in Israel's interest and the Palestinian peoples' interest, but that is one.

I also think there is another good news story maybe, and that is Tunisia, where an Islamist party, the Ennahda party, won the first election and has now in a peace deal with other parties surrendered power to a coalition, and just maybe that can show some success.

So, I think a lot of what you said is very true, but I think there are ways—and our vigilance and focus will be necessary—that progress can be made.

Mr. LIEBERMAN. I will just add briefly, thanks for your statement. So it was a thought-provoking statement.

In my opinion, we do have friends in the countries throughout the Middle East who essentially share our goals, that what is happening—and we won't have any friends if we just pull back. They are not asking, as General Keane said, for the U.S. Army to be or the military to be on the ground. They are asking for our help, and what is happening now, after the so-called Arab Spring, is really a remarkable historic development in the Arab world, which is an uprising against dictators, autocrats, by the people. They want freedom and they want a better opportunity to make some more money for their families, and in almost every case, these revolutions have been led by the under- or unemployed children of the middle class, who are well-educated, who understood how much better things could be.

What is happening now in some of these countries in the conflicts that the revolutions have unleashed is not dissimilar to what has happened before when autocrats or totalitarian regimes are overthrown. They unleash this kind of conflict. It happened in Eastern Europe, Central Europe. In some sense, that is what happened in Bosnia-Herzegovina, but if we stand back, it is only going to get worse.

I will—I know the Sunni-Shia conflict has been going on for a millennia-plus, but I also know that there is a lot of mixing between Sunnis and Shias throughout the Middle East, and this is, as you said, it is not a zero-sum game. We ought to be able to work out a system, and Tunisia is the hopeful example where everybody could feel that there is a way for them to win. Frankly, as we have said earlier over and over, it is in our interest to see that happen, not only because it reflects our best National values, but it also reflects what is best for our security.

Mr. JONES. If I could just very briefly follow up with two points.

One is I would just, on your Northern Ireland example, I think one of the useful lessons the United States is now in is the shift the British had, the mindset shifting from a heavy military footprint to target the IRA to one that was much lighter, focused on MI5 and the Royal Ulster Constabulary, that allowed a peace process to even be possible, in part because the IRA was so weakened by that point.

The other thing I would say, just to reiterate, is we do have allies. We don't have common interests across the board with all of them. We do have allies that hate extremism. If you look at the progress that has been made in Somalia, tossing out Shabaab from Mogadishu, from Kismayo, tossing out extremists from other areas, we do have allies. We do have allies, local populations in Mali that hate extremism. So I think in that sense we have to gravitate towards those kinds of organizations.

General KEANE. You know, I think it is a thoughtful question and one that has been asked before. I think it is just too simplistic to categorize the entire Middle East as a conflict between Sunnis and Shias, a sectarian conflict. I am not minimizing the fact that it exists, I think you have to understand it does exist, but what is happening there is there are authoritarian regimes, every single one of them, except for Israel, and the drivers of instability as a result of these authoritarian regimes are the lack of political and social justice and the lack of economic opportunity. As a result of that, the radical Islamists use that and leverage that to gain support for what they are attempting to do.

So we have to look at the region and see what has taken place in that region and how this very ambitious political movement that is trying to drive us out of the region so they can have their way—and that is what 9/11 was all about, it was about driving us out of the region, it is one of their major strategic objectives—and for us to make certain that that region doesn't explode with this radical Islamic movement, which would not only threaten the region but the world at large. They are a world domination objective organization. It is hard for us to get our head around that intellectually, I think, but nonetheless that is their idea, not ours.

So the only answer here is to work this, I think, comprehensively—what are you trying to achieve here, is what I would love the administration to articulate—and then individually work with partners in the region to deal with the realities that they have. Some of these realities are dealing with our allies, Mr. Congressman, who are authoritarian regimes, who are repressive in dealing with their people, the lack of social justice that exists in these regions. Yet we have harmonious relationships with them that are financially rewarding. The fact of the matter is we should be leveraging these regimes to move in a different direction.

That is why I am saying it is not just kinetic. What is our strategy, what we are trying to do? I am not suggesting we force democracy on everybody. But I am suggesting that if you focus on what the drivers of instability are, injustice to people and lack of economic opportunity, you can start to make some progress in the region. Certainly staying engaged is the answer, as opposed to just the sense of futility and hopelessness that we get. The culture is dramatically different from the United States, the geography is harsh, everything about it is hard. It is easy to say, let's just walk away from it. That would be a tragedy, and it would result in harm to the American people.

Chairman MCCAUL. The Chairman now recognizes the Chairman of the Oversight Subcommittee, Mr. Duncan.

Mr. DUNCAN. Thank you, Mr. Chairman. Thanks for having this very insightful hearing today.

First off, I want to add my voice to the thanks to Senator Lieberman and Congresswoman Harman for your service to our country.

General, for your service in the 101st Airborne, 10th Mountain Division, 1st Brigade. The Chairman and I were able to visit with the 3rd Brigade Combat Team in Afghanistan in November 2011, and the memories that I have of the men and women that are serving in harm's way go a long way. I just want to thank everyone that is serving to fight and counter the elements that we are talking about today around the globe, whether it is in the southern Philippines or Afghanistan or where it may be.

Senator Lieberman, I want to also thank you for some comments in your opening statement, when you said, let me underscore here the enemy is violent Islamist extremism, a political ideology that seeks to justify totalitarian governance by perverting religion. The enemy, we can never stress enough, is not Islam itself, it is the Islamist extremists that use religion for its own use and gain.

So I want to shift gears from some of the topics that we have talked about today, because talking about a false narrative that endangers the homeland, and as I sat here and listened to some of the testimony I thought about the false narrative with respect to our Nation's borders. That is the use of the term "operational control," and that we have a secure Southern Border.

So I want to ask each of you, in your opinion, how does border security, specifically the Southern Border in this instance, but we can't limit it just to the Southern Border. We have a long Northern Border with huge ports of entry. We have ocean and seaports, airports that are all playing into that border security element. So how does National border security play into your thoughts with regard to National security countering al-Qaeda elements, countering any other threats, but also the false narrative of an operational control element? So I will start with Senator Lieberman.

Mr. LIEBERMAN. Thanks, Congressman. Thanks for your kind words. Let me begin the discussion. I have been out for about a year, so I don't know the latest. But part of the challenge post-9/11 was not just the security-privacy tension, but how do we maintain security in a country that has historically been as open as ours, and that includes the geographical fate of America which has always protected us? We are surrounded by two oceans, we have historically friendly allies to the north and south. We have enormous borders. You are never going to really maintain full security unless you do your best on those borders.

I think we have come a long way since 9/11 toward achieving that. We are probably doing better at airport and airline security than we are at some other places. We have improved, I think, our ability at points of entry on the north and the south borders to stop people that want to do us harm from coming in. The Southern Border is obviously a unique problem because of the enormous flows of people across that border, including, obviously, illegal immigrants.

So, bottom line, if you are talking about homeland security, you have got to in the post 9/11 age protect your borders, all of them, air, sea, land. We have done a lot better. But this is one of those journeys that doesn't have an end point, we are just going to keep having to do better and better.

Mr. DUNCAN. Right. Let me just, before I go to Congresswoman Harman, let me just remind everyone that Hezbollah has exploited our Southern Border.

Mr. LIEBERMAN. That is correct.

Mr. DUNCAN. So Ms. Harman.

Ms. HARMAN. Thank you. I think it is an important question. This committee should take a victory lap for its authorship of the Safe Ports Act about 5 years ago. It was a bipartisan law that passed the House and Senate, was signed I think by President Bush. I think it predates President Obama. But what we did is push our borders out. We thought about how important it is to inspect cargo, for example, at the point of embarkation on ships and then to lock down those ships, and then of course to have security at the actual ports of entry. But we called it layered security. That layered security approach is now the approach that we take at our airports as well in a variety of ways. So there really should be an appreciation of that.

On the physical land borders, Canada and the Southern Border, I would just point out that so far as I know, and again I may be a little stale, more terrorists have tried to enter our country through the Canadian border than through the Southern Border. That doesn't mean the Southern Border doesn't matter; of course it does. But one of the early bad guys that an astute I think customs official was able to spot was a guy named Ahmed Ressam, who was trying to cross the Canadian border in Washington State with a rental car full of explosives. His intended target was LAX, then in my Congressional district. So of course I would remember that and think it was a heroic act to have stopped the guy.

But, yes, looking at all the borders, as you have described, should be, should remain a high priority. But let's not forget that homegrown terrorists who are already here, many of them legally, are getting radicalized on the internet, but also by live people in their neighborhoods, and we have to keep a focus on that.

Mr. DUNCAN. Absolutely.

General, can you give a military perspective on that real quickly?

General KEANE. Well, from our perspective, I think what our intelligence agencies have done to thwart terrorism is really notable since 9/11 and the cooperation that these agencies have.

I am convinced in my own mind that no amount of fencing in and of itself is going to stop a determined terrorist from getting into this country. What we have do is stay focused on them. We have to be into their phone conversations, we have to be into their internet, we have to know what their thinking is, and we have to stop those kind of activities before they start.

So our intelligence services, yes, the National Security Agency, the extraordinary work that they have been able to do is really critical to stopping this. Do we need a secure border in the southern part of the United States, given all the problems associated with it? Certainly, we do. As Congresswoman mentioned, the focus we have taken and the layered approach where it begins overseas is really critical for us. We have had a lot of success as a result of it. So the resources that are necessary for that kind of work is something that you are all doing and I applaud you for it.

Mr. JONES. I think one of the more interesting discussions on this came from the bin Laden documents from the Abbottabad compound, where senior al-Qaeda leaders noted two things I would highlight on the subject. One is frustration at the closed borders and the progress the United States had made in making it more difficult for them to get inside, actually hearing it from senior leaders themselves. But also the commitment of finding and exploiting ways to get inside of the homeland, whether it was individuals, as bin Laden had said at one point, trying to get somebody with a Mexican visa that they could smuggle through the Southern Border or elsewhere.

Look, we have had people leave the United States and go to train with militant groups overseas, senior levels of al-Shabaab, Syrians, other locations, Afghanistan as well, and Pakistan. We have had people that have come back and been involved in plots and we had not discovered them. Zazi, Shahzad, Abdulmutallab were all back in the United States when they were involved in plots.

Mr. DUNCAN. The Boston bombers.

Mr. JONES. Exactly. The Boston bombers. So this will remain a problem.

I think the issue with our border security has got to be border security is good up until the point that it has useful intelligence. I think one of the aspects about this then is—and this is where Syria comes back into the picture—we are only as good as people whose names we have access to and we can pass to folks in the border security. One concern I have had in talking to folks that we have working in and around Syria is we don't know all the people over there. We know many of them, but not all of them. If those names don't get on lists, they don't get back to border security, they can come in or out without being stopped.

So I would then fuse those two issues of border security and intelligence as being crucial and potentially vulnerable if we don't have access to that information.

Mr. DUNCAN. Thank you for your time.

Mr. Chairman, I want to point the committee to an article in the Weekly Standard by Thomas Joscelyn, "Know Your Enemy, al-Qaeda's Grand Strategy." I would like to enter this for the record.

Chairman McCAUL. Without objection, so ordered.

[The information follows:]

49

ARTICLE SUBMITTED FOR THE RECORD BY HONORABLE JEFF DUNCAN

JANUARY 20, 2014

KNOW YOUR ENEMY: AL QAEDA'S GRAND STRATEGY [1]

By THOMAS JOSCELYN

In the summer of 2008, Barack Obama, senator and presidential candidate, toured the war zones of Afghanistan and Iraq. Obama had endeared himself to the antiwar left by denouncing President Bush's decision to topple Saddam Hussein and repeatedly claiming that the war in Iraq had diverted resources from defeating al Qaeda and its allies in South Asia. Obama did not tone down this criticism even as he spoke with CBS News from Kabul on July 20, shortly before proceeding to Saddam's former abode. "We got distracted by Iraq," Obama said. Afghanistan "has to be the central focus, the central front [in] our battle against terrorism."

Some top U.S. military commanders, including General David Petraeus, then the face of the American war effort, disagreed with Obama's assessment. And in Iraq, the general and the senator squared off. The contentious meeting between Petraeus and Obama has been recorded in *The Endgame: The Inside Story of the Struggle for Iraq,* from George W. Bush to Barack Obama, by *New York Times* reporter Michael Gordon and General Bernard E. Trainor.

Obama repeated that "Afghanistan is the central front in the war on terror," and therefore a timetable for withdrawing troops from Iraq was necessary. Petraeus disagreed: "Actually, Senator, Iraq is what al Qaeda says is the central front."

Obama was unpersuaded. "The Al-Qaeda leadership is not here in Iraq. They are there," Obama said, pointing to Pakistan on a map.

Petraeus, of course, knew this. The general did not need the senator to point out the obvious. And besides, Petraeus argued, Obama was missing the point. Whatever one thought of the decision to invade Saddam's neo-Stalinist state in the first place, al Qaeda had made the fight for Iraq its main priority.

Obama pressed forward, questioning "whether Al Qaeda in Iraq [AQI] presented a threat to the United States," Gordon and Trainor write. "If AQI has morphed into a kind of mafia then they are not going to be blowing up buildings," Obama said. Petraeus pointed to a failed terrorist attack in Scotland in 2007 as an example of why Obama's thinking was wrong. "Well, think about the Glasgow airport," Petraeus warned. The general, according to Gordon and Trainor, "also noted the potential of AQI to expand its influence to Syria and Lebanon."

The debate between Obama and Petraeus may seem like ancient history after more than five years have passed. And Obama went on to "end" the war in Iraq, or so he claimed during his reelection campaign and thereafter, by withdrawing all of America's forces at the end of 2011.

The truth, however, is that the disagreement between Obama and Petraeus still resonates today. Al Qaeda has come roaring back in Iraq, capturing significant territory in Fallujah, Ramadi, and elsewhere. Obama does not believe this is a major concern. And, just as Petraeus warned, AQI has "expanded its influence" in neighboring Syria as a result of the revolution against Bashar al-Assad. Other al Qaeda affiliates have joined AQI in the fight for Syria.

But there is something even more fundamental about the Obama-Petraeus debate. It goes to the heart of how we define al Qaeda itself.

More than a dozen years since the September 11, 2001, terrorist attacks, the United States is still confused about al Qaeda's goals and even how the group founded by Osama bin Laden is organized. The intellectual confusion is pervasive—and some of it is deliberate.

Political Revolutionaries

Osama bin Laden will always be remembered for his success in attacking the United States within its own borders, thereby shattering Americans' illusion of security. To this day, if you listen to many commentators, this is al Qaeda's principal reason for existence. It is widely thought that if al Qaeda is not striking targets in the West, then the group must be close to defeat. This is simply not true.

Terrorizing the United States and its Western allies was always a tactic, a step toward achieving al Qaeda's real goal—power for its leaders and their ideology in the heart of the Islamic world. Al Qaeda's jihadists are not just terrorists; they are political revolutionaries. They have sought, since al Qaeda's founding in 1988, to overturn the existing political order in various Muslim-ruled countries.

[1] *http://www.weeklystandard.com/articles/know-your-enemy__774088.html?nopager=1.*

Al Qaeda's ideologues believed that the status quo before the 2011 Arab uprisings was heretical. They believed that Muslim rulers had abandoned true Islam by neglecting to implement sharia law as defined by al Qaeda. They also believed, and continue to believe, that an imaginary Zionist-Crusader conspiracy has prevented the real believers from achieving success. Therefore, al Qaeda deduced, the conspirators must be confronted.

By striking America, al Qaeda's most senior leaders believed, they could cause the U.S. government eventually to withdraw its support for various Muslim rulers and Israel. According to bin Laden and other al Qaeda thinkers, American support was the main reason why early jihadist efforts to overthrow Muslim dictatorships ended in bloody fiascos.

Strike America, al Qaeda argued, and it will crumble just as the Soviets did after their embarrassing loss to the mujahedeen in Afghanistan in the 1980s. As America's influence wanes, al Qaeda's theory of the world continued, the apostate tyrants who rule throughout the Muslim world will become susceptible to the jihadists' revolution. Al Qaeda and like-minded jihadists can then replace the dictators with pure Islamic states based on sharia law. And these states can then link up to resurrect the Caliphate, a supranational Islamic empire that was dissolved in 1924 and that has taken on a mythical status in al Qaeda's thinking.

This is how al Qaeda has long seen the world and why America was struck on September 11, 2001. It is why U.S. interests were attacked well before 9/11 and have continued to be targeted ever since. Al Qaeda's conspiratorial view of Middle Eastern politics, its deep hatred of the West, and its resentment of Western influence in the Islamic world made such attacks necessary.

Al Qaeda has repeatedly made this strategy clear. In his 2002 letter to the American people, Osama bin Laden emphasized that "our fight against these [Muslim] governments is not separate from our fight against you." Removing "these governments is an obligation upon us, and a necessary step to free the Ummah [community of believers], to make the Shariah the supreme law and to regain Palestine."

In private correspondence recovered in bin Laden's Abbottabad compound nine years later, the terror master repeatedly made the same point. Bin Laden emphasized the necessity of striking American interests as a step towards building a true Islamic state. Bin Laden worried that, however much the United States had been weakened since 9/11, the world's lone superpower retained the ability to destroy an al Qaeda-style nation should it arise. The "more we can conduct operations against America, the closer we get to uniting our efforts to establish an Islamic State," bin Laden or one of his top lieutenants wrote in 2010. Still, al Qaeda's leaders believed that the "time to establish an Islamic state is near, and the jihadist ideology is spreading abroad."

Al Qaeda adjusted its tactics in the post-9/11 world, especially with American troops on the ground in Iraq and Afghanistan. Bin Laden wrote in another letter that his organization must "concentrate" its "jihad efforts in areas where the conditions are ideal for us to fight." Bin Laden concluded that "Iraq and Afghanistan are two good examples."

The centrality of the Iraq war, from al Qaeda's perspective, was emphasized in a letter from Ayman al Zawahiri, then bin Laden's top deputy, to the head of Al Qaeda in Iraq in 2005. Zawahiri wrote: "I want to be the first to congratulate you for what God has blessed you with in terms of fighting in the heart of the Islamic world, which was formerly the field for major battles in Islam's history, and what is now the place for the greatest battle of Islam in this era."

The very fight that Barack Obama has long seen as tangential to al Qaeda's operations, and even similar to Mafia-style crime, was viewed quite differently by al Qaeda's leaders. It was the "greatest battle of Islam in this era."

This was not empty rhetoric. Numerous public and private statements from al Qaeda emphasized the centrality of Iraq and their desire to establish an Islamic state in the heart of the Middle East.

Al Qaeda has continued to adjust its operations in the wake of the 2011 Arab uprisings. In Syria, the organization has devoted a substantial amount of its resources to defeating Bashar al-Assad's regime and establishing a new Islamic regime. Elsewhere, in countries ruled by newly installed Islamist governments, such as Tunisia, al Qaeda initially advised jihadists to refrain from fighting altogether. In such countries it was best, al Qaeda said, to concentrate on recruiting and to build a base of popular support for its ideology. Over time, that strategy has evolved, however, as the Tunisian government has cracked down on al Qaeda-allied organizations.

But everywhere, the goal is the same: to advance a political revolution that al Qaeda sparked more than a quarter of a century ago.

Al Qaeda's Global Network

Once you understand al Qaeda's true aspirations, the structure of its organization begins to make sense. Although much of al Qaeda's network remains clandestine, a vast amount of information on its operations is available to the public.

The days when al Qaeda was a small cadre have long since passed. From its earliest days, al Qaeda devoted a substantial share of its efforts to insurgencies ranging from Chechnya to North Africa. Before 9/11, most of the recruits who passed through al Qaeda-sponsored training camps in Afghanistan were tasked with doing something other than attacking America. "Some experts even believe that the ratio of insurgent fighters to terrorists in al Qaeda's camps may be 15 to 1," notes the START Database's website, which is sponsored by the U.S. Department of Homeland Security. This created a deep well from which al Qaeda could draw manpower. Estimates of the number of jihadists trained in al Qaeda's camps prior to 9/11 vary, but easily totaled 10,000. (U.S. intelligence estimates cited by the 9/11 Commission range from 10,000 to 20,000 fighters. Other estimates are much higher.) Only 19 of these trainees attacked the United States on 9/11.

Going back to his days in Sudan in the early 1990s, bin Laden believed that his al Qaeda was the vanguard of the global jihadist movement. According to the 9/11 Commission, bin Laden "had a vision of himself as head of an international jihad confederation." Bin Laden established an "Islamic Army Shura," which "was to serve as the coordinating body for the consortium of terrorist groups with which he was forging alliances." The Shura "was composed of his own al Qaeda Shura together with leaders or representatives of terrorist organizations that were still independent." As of the early 1990s, bin Laden and al Qaeda pursued a "pattern of expansion through building alliances" and thus had laid the "groundwork for a true global terrorist network."

Throughout the 1990s and thereafter, al Qaeda continued to pursue versions of this original vision. In some cases, other jihadist groups were outright absorbed into bin Laden's joint venture. In other instances, al Qaeda remained closely allied with jihadist organizations that did not formally merge with it. Al Qaeda also deliberately spawned new groups to expand its influence.

Al Qaeda's policy of aggressive geographic expansion has been largely successful of late. While the group once relied almost entirely on a network of secret operatives embedded within countries ruled by hostile governments, al Qaeda now has formal branches (often called "affiliates") operating in Africa, throughout the Middle East, and in South Asia. Each branch is fighting to create an Islamic state and has openly declared its loyalty to Ayman al Zawahiri, bin Laden's successor as the head of al Qaeda.

Al Qaeda in the Arabian Peninsula (AQAP) is headquartered in Yemen and led by Nasir al Wuhayshi, Osama bin Laden's former protégé. In August 2013, Zawahiri appointed Wuhayshi as the general manager of al Qaeda's global operations. This gives Wuhayshi great power across the network. Wuhayshi has been experimenting with al Qaeda-style governance, even creating a new brand (Ansar al Sharia, or Defenders of Sharia) for his efforts. Ansar al Sharia in Yemen was the first of several similarly named jihadist groups to emerge following the Arab uprisings.

Al Qaeda in the Islamic Maghreb (AQIM) took over much of Mali in 2012 until the French intervened in January 2013. The group continues to operate throughout West and North Africa. In Somalia, another al Qaeda branch, Al Shabaab, continues to hold some territory and wage an insurgency against African forces.

The war in Syria has been a boon for al Qaeda. Jabhat al Nusra and the Islamic State of Iraq and Syria, the successor to Al Qaeda in Iraq, have thousands of fighters on the ground in Syria and Iraq. The two have quarreled over leadership and other matters. But they are still doing a considerable amount of damage while probably controlling more territory than al Qaeda has ever held before. There are other al Qaeda-allied groups operating inside Syria as well.

In addition to these five official branches, there are numerous jihadist groups that have said they are part of al Qaeda's global jihad. And in South Asia, al Qaeda continues to operate as part of a terror "syndicate," owing to its decades-long ties to extremist organizations that share its ideology. Al Qaeda continues to cooperate closely with the Taliban, Lashkar-e-Taiba, and an alphabet soup of other groups based in Pakistan. They are jointly seeking to re-establish the Taliban's Islamic state in Afghanistan.

The degree of command and control exercised by al Qaeda's senior leaders over this global network is hotly debated. But the minimalists have to ignore a substantial body of evidence showing that Zawahiri and his lieutenants maintain a significant amount of influence, despite the management problems that any human organization faces.

The Enemy Gets a Vote

The debate between Obama and Petraeus in 2008 has not been resolved. If anything, Obama now defines al Qaeda more narrowly than ever before, even as al Qaeda's many branches have become more virulent.

To hear the Obama administration explain the current state of the war, you would never know that al Qaeda seeks to establish Islamic states, or that the group has made stunning advances toward this end. Instead, the president and his surrogates consistently draw a hard line between al Qaeda's "core" in South Asia and "affiliated" groups everywhere else. Some are quick to brand virtually any jihadist group, even if it is openly pro-al Qaeda and has well-known ties to one or more of al Qaeda's branches, as a "local" nuisance that should not be considered part of al Qaeda's network. Such arguments miss the entire reason for al Qaeda's existence, which has always been to acquire power in "local" settings. This is why al Qaeda has always devoted most of its resources to fueling insurgencies.

It would be naive to assume that the Obama administration's definition of al Qaeda is not directly tied to its preferred policies. President Obama is dedicated to decreasing the American military's footprint, even as al Qaeda has increased its own. U.S. troops were pulled out of Iraq by the end of 2011. And a short-lived surge of forces in Afghanistan was ended, with the goal of removing most of America's forces in the near future. While Obama argued in 2008 that Afghanistan, not Iraq, must be our "central front," it quickly became apparent that this was political rhetoric, not a real strategy. Drone strikes, Special Forces raids, and other covert activities are sufficient, in the Obama administration's view.

This is not to suggest that large-scale American military deployments are necessary everywhere al Qaeda's branches prosper. But in the coming months, there simply will be no central front in America's fight against al Qaeda and its allies.

President Obama's plan for fighting al Qaeda, therefore, rests on a gamble. As long as al Qaeda's various branches do not successfully attack the continental United States, then the United States will not treat them as first-order security threats. In countries where America has semi-reliable allies, others will take the fight to al Qaeda. In countries where no allied forces exist, such as Syria, America and the West will simply hope for the best. Well over 100,000 Syrians have been killed since the uprising against Assad's regime began; thousands of them have been killed by al Qaeda's branches. In Obama's estimation, al Qaeda's victims inside Syria and Iraq are not America's concern.

But there are already indications that Obama's understanding of the enemy cannot be sustained. Al Qaeda's branches, especially Al Qaeda in the Arabian Peninsula (AQAP), and closely allied groups, such as the Pakistani Taliban, now threaten the U.S. homeland. The threats to American security from al Qaeda's global network are multiplying, not receding.

And during a press briefing on October 30, an anonymous senior White House official explained to reporters that Al Qaeda in Iraq and Syria is "really a transnational threat network" now. "This is really a major and increasing threat to Iraq's stability, it's [an] increasing threat to our regional partners, and it's an increasing threat to us," the official continued.

That is, General Petraeus had a point about Iraq all along.

Meanwhile, al Qaeda strives on towards its real goal. It is a difficult course, and success is far from certain. But history tells us that a lot of carnage can be wrought in pursuit of violent fantasies.

In one of the documents recovered in his Abbottabad compound, Osama bin Laden wrote that "the jihad war is ongoing, and on several fronts." The strategy is simple: "Once America is weak, we can build our Muslim state."

Chairman MCCAUL. Chair recognizes my colleague from Texas to wrap up this hearing, Mr. O'Rourke.

Mr. O'ROURKE. Thank you, Mr. Chairman.

I am certainly no apologist for the administration's National security strategy, and I have some significant concerns with it. But a lack of focus or vigor in the prosecution of the war on terror are not among them. And if you look at the unprecedented level of both domestic and international surveillance that have come to light recently—the drone strikes against terrorist targets who present a direct threat to this country, and also targets who are the enemies of our allies that don't present a direct threat to this country, the surge of forces in Afghanistan in the first term of this administration, and as has been mentioned before, the killing of bin Laden—it is hard to see how one could reach the conclusion that there is a lack of focus or interest or intent to successfully prosecute the war on terror in this administration.

To General Keane's point, to use his phrase, that the mess in Iraq is the result of—again, his word—the bungling of the administration's negotiators in Iraq, I reach a different conclusion. I think that, to use that word, the mess we are in is a result of our invasion of that country in the first place, the lack of critical questions to the assumptions that we made prior to that invasion, and the inability to think through the consequences of that invasion.

So I hear a lot of military solutions to the very complex terrorism problems and threats that our country faces in the Middle East. I would love to hear, General Keane, Senator Lieberman, Congresswoman Harman, Dr. Jones, if there is time, like to hear you reflect on some of the perhaps unintended consequences of military action, of invasions, of military presence in the Middle East, of drone strikes, and what those activities do to perhaps increase the threat or complicate the threat that we have over there.

Again to use General Keane's, I think, excellent idea of what that might mean to a comprehensive strategy beyond a military presence or a remainder of forces in Afghanistan and Iraq. I guess I would like to start with Senator Lieberman.

Mr. LIEBERMAN. Thanks. Thanks, Congressman.

So I would say that the positive aspects of the Obama administration's record in counterterrorism that you stated I agree with. But what I am saying here, and I will go back to what I said earlier, is that in many other ways what the administration is doing is not working. In other words, if we are not helping the moderates, nonextremists in Syria, if we are sitting back now as Iraq becomes a sanctuary for al-Qaeda, if we are doing the same essentially in Libya, if we are going to let Afghanistan basically go the way that Iraq did and not have an agreement to leave any troops there by the end of this year, we are inviting the whirlwind.

So what I am saying is not to criticize the positive things you have said, but essentially to say, Mr. President, there are 3 more years in which you are going to be our commander-in-chief. A lot of what you are now doing, in my respectful opinion, is simply not working to protect our security, and it is diminishing our credibility in areas of the world way outside of the Middle East.

I talk to people in Asia. I was just in Asia about a month ago. The world is small. When they see us pulling back from, well, countries that think are our close allies in the Middle East, they read it personally. They think, wow, what is going to happen if China makes a move on me? Can I rely on the United States? They think they can't.

So I join you, and, as I said in my opening statement, appreciating what the Obama administration has done, including particularly here at home in supporting the Homeland Security Department and the various elements of National security that were adopted post-9/11. But I think there are large parts of the foreign policy approach of the administration that are simply not working and——

Mr. O'ROURKE. Senator Lieberman, excuse me. Respectfully.

Mr. LIEBERMAN. Go ahead.

Mr. O'ROURKE. But I guess to one of the points I was attempting to make: Do you acknowledge that there is another side to the more aggressive, robust presence that you and General Keane have been arguing for, and acknowledging it doesn't mean that you dispute its total or net value, but that a presence there also serves al-Qaeda's interests in being able to recruit additional people, drone strikes help in their recruiting? Again, not to argue against them, but to say that it is a much more complex picture and that more aggression or a greater or more robust presence doesn't necessarily mean that there aren't complications.

Mr. LIEBERMAN. Yes, of course, there are. I mean, this is the complication of life in a very dangerous world. But the bottom line here is, and General Keane was right earlier when he said this is going to go on for a large part of this century. We are facing a group of people, violent Islamist extremists. They represent a distinct minority in the Islamic world. And yet they are fearless, they are an ideologically-driven killing machine, killing mostly Muslims. So, yes, a lot of the things we have done will have a counterreaction. But in the end, if we do nothing, the result will be worse.

Again I think we have all said it today, none of us are calling for hundreds of thousands of troops back into Syria, Iraq, Afghanistan. But, you know, you can overlearn the lessons of the last war. One of them would be to just pull out because the consequences of that would be disastrous for our country and our people.

Mr. O'ROURKE. Thank you.

Ms. HARMAN. I applaud your patience in sitting here for 2½ hours. We are also patient. We are the witnesses.

Mr. LIEBERMAN. We were all each once the junior member of our committee.

Ms. HARMAN. Yeah. Many stories to tell.

Mr. LIEBERMAN. We identify with your pain.

Ms. HARMAN. I also applaud your question. I don't think anyone here is saying let's cut and run from the Middle East, if that is the area we are talking about. There are different nuances to what each of us is saying. So here is what I am saying. I am saying we need to continue a robust counterterrorism presence in the Middle East. But that does not mean that we have to have troops everywhere. We can have an over-the-horizon force in some places which we can stage into areas if we need to, to protect U.S. interests. That is one. I am saying we need a robust set of laws that allow us to do what we are all talking about, which is to learn the plans and intentions of bad guys and prevent and disrupt them from attacking us. That is another thing that we need to do.

But just take Iraq. President Obama, as everybody knows, ran on a platform that he would disengage us militarily from Iraq. Many people in America in both parties support this. There is a democratically-elected leader of Iraq who is supposed to represent the whole population, not just the Shia population, and that is an issue. I think John Kerry is right in calling on Maliki to represent his entire population and to provide leadership.

Similarly in Afghanistan, they are not the same country, not the same set of problems, but there is an elected leader. There hopefully will be a reasonably fair election. I am not optimistic because the last one was so unfair. But I think it is important that the countries themselves exercise leadership as we try to help them.

My final point is, at least speaking for me, we should never disengage from that region. The history of every major religion is there, many of our allies are there. It is important to keep brain cells on the problem. But it is also important to continually revise the strategies that we use. I applaud especially Secretary Kerry for trying to do that.

Mr. O'ROURKE. Thank you.

General KEANE. Well, that is an excellent commentary, and I welcome the opportunity to respond to it.

When you take a look at Iraq and Afghanistan and you look at troop presence and what happened there, the fact of the matter is until we got the right strategy in Iraq—I am not going to reargue should we or should we not have gone to Iraq. I have views on that as well. But the fact of the matter is, we were there, and we finally applied a counterinsurgency strategy which was designed to protect the people. Once the people saw that we were willing to die, and die we did, protecting them, something we had not done up to that point, and the Iraqis did not have the capability to do it, the war turned to our favor.

Also strangely at the same time the al-Qaeda had fallen in on Iraq because of our presence. That is a true statement. So that was a huge negative outcome as a result of the invasion of Iraq. Al-Qaeda fell in on Iraq because they saw it as a huge opportunity to render a defeat to the United States. They feared strategically the United States would possibly turn Iraq into a country that had democratic principles and economic opportunity, something that they ideologically are fundamentally opposed to.

But their message is so harsh and their means are so brutal that the Sunnis themselves rejected them, even though they were supporting them for 3 years. We would never have had the success we had with the surge, with the increase of forces applied differently, if we did not have the so-called awakening that took place with the Sunni tribal leaders who were rejecting the al-Qaeda, the brutality of 7th century Talibanism that they enforced upon them. So we have to understand that, that this message that they bring to Muslims is a very harsh, strident message, and we can leverage against that.

In Afghanistan, and I have been there 15, 20 times, the people themselves, when you free the people from the harshness and brutality of the Taliban, we don't have to win their hearts and minds, all we have to do is kill the bad guy who is terrorizing them and just driving their life into the gutter. Once we do that, the people are very supportive of us.

So my point to you is, is this cancer is out there, and we have the means to deal with some of it. Most of it has to be dealt with, with those countries. In doing that, I think we can help them intellectually to deal this, we can help them in terms of the kinds of government they have, in terms of improving those governments and the needs for their people. If you want to be an ally of the United States, then these are some of the conditions that we want to see.

Also certainly we can go a long way with helping—we have learned an awful lot, Congressman about how to deal with this militarily. We forgot the lessons of Vietnam. That is one of the reasons why we had such a problem with this initially in Afghanistan and also in Iraq. But now we understand how to do this. We can truly help our partners in the region when they have to use military force, this gets you the best results in using that military force.

So there is so much that we can do. I think it is learning the lessons that we have learned from the mistakes that we have made and applying those lessons and partnering and staying engaged. When we pull back, the enemy moves forward. That is what has happened right before our eyes. You know, the government in Libya is a moderate government, friendly to the United States. You know what they want from us? To provide assistance to train a proper security force so that they can disarm the militias and be a counterbalance against the al-Qaeda radical Islamist threat. That is what they want. That is small for us, I think, to assist in. The payoff is enormous. Are we doing that? No. And that is tragic, in my view.

Mr. O'ROURKE. Thanks.

Mr. JONES. Very briefly, I think you have put your finger, Congressman, on an important issue, and we have to think about the costs and benefits of how we intervene. There are costs.

I would say, big picture, my concern is that the rebalancing—we heard this from General Keane earlier—the rebalancing to Asia and, in my view, the underfunded support to a U.S. Africa Command that has a very big problem on its hand, do cause some risk. Our decisions on Syria, future decisions on Afghanistan put us in a position where we may take on, in my view, risk.

But I do think you are putting your finger on an important issue, which is, are there costs to how we intervene? I think the answer is yes. I think we have demonstrated that there are types and numbers of forces that can radicalize populations. I think some of the strikes that we have seen overseas when they have killed civilians, especially excessively, have tended to be more harmful than helpful. I would not deny that there have been strikes that have actually been quite helpful and saved American lives.

But you can also overdo it. You can also assume that a drone campaign is the solution. It is an instrument. It is not the solution in and of itself. So I think when you look at this you have got to also see some of the benefits to intervention. I think we are at the position really where we are talking about a much lighter presence overseas, limited, one that includes not just military, but Treasury, State Department, and other officials, and one that does increasingly work with allies in doing this with us, in some cases for us. That is intervention, in my view, that is worth the cost.

Mr. O'ROURKE. Thank you.

Thank you, Mr. Chairman.

Chairman McCAUL. The Chairman now recognizes the gentleman from Pennsylvania, Mr. Perry.

Mr. PERRY. Thank you, Mr. Chairman.

I am sure you are all happy to see me show up. I can assure I was watching the hearing from the office. I had a couple other things and got a little bit of a cold here.

I want to start with Dr. Jones. In your opening statement you kind of alluded to and maybe you need to clarify increased or continued monitoring or surveillance of all Americans for the sake of making sure that we catch or keep track of these al-Qaeda folks. I guess from my viewpoint it seems to me it would be, in a time of limited resources and in a place where our Constitution guarantees our liberties, that the best thing to do is to target specifically individuals, whatever the matrix is, whatever the metrics are, who travel to these places, who correspond with these folks, who live in communities that have a proclivity towards radicalization. I just want to get your thoughts on that, because to me that seems like the better approach.

Also, if you could, to clarify maybe your thoughts on why we are doing the opposite, why we are looking at every single American for the sake of a few who would be bad actors, and is it from a standpoint of political correctness? Or why do we refuse to face this enemy head-on and target our energies and our resources?

Mr. JONES. Sure. Just to be clear, I did not support monitoring all Americans, and I don't believe I said that either. But I did support having a capacity to be able to monitor extremists.

Here is the challenge, though, and this is why this is not a black-and-white issue, a zero-sum issue, is because we can't know and we won't know everybody that has access on the internet and radicalizes. We won't know everybody that goes overseas. There are a range of individuals that may radicalize inside the United States, stay here.

Mr. PERRY. But I would say also, as far as I know, we have no proof of anyone, even a lone wolf, and even under the Patriot Act provisions which haven't been used regarding a lone wolf ever, who has ever been radicalized in the United States solely on their own. In other words, they have had contact with through one means or another, the internet or what-have-you. If the NSA has the capability and the ability, and I think they do, to monitor every single thing we do, that we can and should know that.

I mean, Nidal Hasan was looking at websites that were known, corresponding with bad actors that were known, yet we did absolute nothing. Instead we are spending all this money watching all of us Americans. I guarantee you the only time I have traveled to places that are unsavory were not because I wanted to take my family on a vacation or myself to Afghanistan or the Middle East where there is a civil war going on. People that go to those places I think that they probably would not object to being suspect for their motives. I think that that is where we should be focusing our efforts.

Mr. JONES. I agree. I would point out that you don't have to travel overseas anymore to get the kind of expertise we are talking about.

Mr. PERRY. Sure. But do you correspond, somehow or another, you do correspond with people that are known.

Mr. JONES. You do correspond.

Mr. PERRY. To me, that is where we should be focusing our efforts as opposed to this broad approach to every American. I guarantee the people on my staff, you know, they have never traveled to these countries and they don't correspond with people that are engaged in these kind of things. So spending resources on them is a waste of time, energy, and resources.

Senator would you like to——

Mr. LIEBERMAN. Yeah. Thanks, Congressman. So let me get into this because a lot of people ask this question. In my opinion, part of what you are talking about is the so-called metadata that the NSA goes after. That is one excellent way in which we can get to target. In other words, Congress established a law here, which, incidentally, though it has been subject to criticism, the Chinese don't have a law like this, the Russians don't have a law like this. We actually tried to create a system where there was due process involved.

As you know, I think the metadata, which is looking at millions and millions of phone calls and emails, it is not the content, it is the connections. That is the way they get to target, when they see the connections. Then they have got to go to court to get a court order. I mean, just think about how crazy that would seem to somebody in China or Russia or to the members of al-Qaeda or Iran.

Mr. PERRY. While I agree with you, Senator, at the same time we were doing this, right, and we didn't pick up, we didn't pick up the Boston bombers, who were corresponding and making those connections. We didn't pick up Nidal Hasan.

Mr. LIEBERMAN. No system is perfect. But, I will tell you, the American Government has stopped a lot of terrorist plots against us because of these methods of surveillance.

I want to say something else, I have been thinking about it lately. Every time I go on the internet to buy something, I am giving up more information than the NSA has gotten from those millions of phone calls and emails that they do metadata surveillance of. I just read an article somewhere in the last few days that there is a service now being sold to stores that sort of tells them where people have been, based on their cell phones, before they come into those stores. You know and I know that when I start to Google something or I go on different internet sites, I am getting advertising that is based on previous sites I have been at. So, you know, the private sector knows a lot more about almost every—every American—than the NSA does unless you have got a hit that raises their suspicion and then they have got to go to court.

So I think it is really important for the Congress to be careful—and the President will announce a program tomorrow—before upsetting this system, which I think has really protected our security.

Ms. HARMAN. If I could just add, I deplore what Edward Snowden did. I don't think he was a whistleblower, and I think he in many respects compromised very important security interests. But I applaud the public debate. Where you are coming from is where a lot of Americans are coming from. I think you probably understand this better than they do. Again, metadata is just a list of phone numbers; it is not names, and it is certainly not content.

But I was here when all these systems came into effect. Initially, the administration, the Bush administration in its first term went around Congress and ignored the Foreign Intelligence Surveillance Act, which I, when I discovered that, was very unhappy about. But then Congress amended FISA to reset the system of checks and balances, and there have not been any abuses.

The President's Advisory Committee has recommended changing Section 215 and stopping the storing of this phone metadata by the Federal Government. One recommendation is to create an independent agency, a second is to push it out and have the phone companies store the data. The President, according to reports, is probably not going to do either because the phone companies have pushed back, and they don't want to store the data. But just as one person observing the debate in the country, it would certainly be acceptable to me if we took that recommendation and pushed the data into the private sector and tried to engage, adopt some of the recommendations that will make the American public more comfortable.

We need a strong surveillance system. But it needs also to give comfort to Americans that their privacy is being respected. I think this debate should lead to changes, and I hope that the President will be forward-leading on Friday when he proposes changes.

Mr. PERRY. I appreciate—my time has long since expired, as you folks know—I appreciate the Chairman's indulgence. I guess my point is that I want us, our policy, our security policy to be targeted on those who would do us harm and do as much as it can to secure our God-given freedoms and our Constitutional freedoms as so enumerated. I appreciate your thoughts and opinions and your testimony today. Thank you.

Chairman MCCAUL. I thank the gentleman.

Let me just say just for the record, when I was a Federal prosecutor we did go to the private phone carriers. It was not amassed under, you know, giant warehouse under the NSA. I think that is what gives the American people some pause, quite frankly. But I do think it has been effective. It is a legal system.

I just want, and I know it is getting late, but as Chairman I want to exercise my prerogative to throw one last question, because we have such great expertise on this panel. I want to thank you for being here today. It has to do with Afghanistan. I am very concerned. General Keane, as you mentioned, the status of forces agreement, we had a failure to negotiate that in Iraq. Now we are looking at al-Qaeda in Iraq taking over Fallujah, taking over large portions of the country. We are faced with that same dilemma now with Afghanistan. I think Karzai's playing a lot of politics with us. Lack of a better word, he is jerking our chain a little bit, trying to play to his local base, if you will, his local politics. There has been some talk of what is called a zero option, which would result in a complete, 100 percent withdrawal from the region.

Can you tell me what impact that zero option, if exercised, would have on our security to the homeland and in our fight against al-Qaeda?

General KEANE. Certainly. Listen, Karzai, as we all know, is a mercurial figure, and he frustrates the daylights out of us for the entire time he has been there, at times. The fact of the matter is, he is going to be gone in the spring. Election is around April. I think from a policy perspective we should not react emotionally to him, although I understand why people would, but look beyond Karzai. There is going to be a new leader in Afghanistan. If we have to sign this with the new leader, so be it, because sign it we must. Certainly we need to keep residual forces there.

Listen, the current situation, just so you get a grasp of the security situation, the surge forces were applied in the south, and it is relatively stable there as a result of that. We did not get all the forces we wanted, we got 75 percent of them, 30 versus 40, and we had to sequentially apply those forces in the north.

The problem was the President pulled those forces out before we could apply them in the north. The original intent was put them in the east—excuse me—and put them in the south, simultaneously take the Taliban down at the same time with surge forces. Only could put them in the south. That situation is relatively stable, and the Afghans are holding their own.

The problem we have is in the east. We never were able to generate the combat power there that we have in the south. As a result of that, we are leaving the Afghans with a bit of a problem, and we know that. The fact of the matter is we also conduct an aggressive counterterrorism program out of Afghanistan bases using the Central Intelligence Agency to do that. We conduct counterterrorism inside Afghanistan using special operations forces to do that against high-value targets. Both of those we need to keep. Both of those would be at risk seriously if we pulled our forces out. It is hard for me to imagine those operations, the Central Intelligence Agency operation being able to, as robust as it is, be conducted there without any of our security forces and intelligence that we are providing for them.

So the situation in Afghanistan as residual forces, there are two other issues. One is we are providing enablers for the Afghan forces. They are essentially an infantry organization. We need to continue to provide some enablers for them, not for 10 years, but at least for a few more years after 2014, until they are able to have that capacity themselves, logistics, intelligence, some communication. Some of the residual force would do that.

Then also we need some trainers and assistance at the headquarters level to help shape the Afghan military's thinking about how to cope with some of the problems. We are not going to have trigger-pullers on the ground side-by-side with them, but just some relatively senior officers and senior NCOs to help them do that. That is probably about 15,000 to 20,000 troops is what we need to do that. We pull that away, all those functions go down the tube, the terrorist operation in Pakistan, which directly relates to the security of the American people, is at risk, and the gains we have made in Afghanistan to date would also be tragically at risk by pulling those forces out.

Chairman MCCAUL. I couldn't agree with you more.

Senator Lieberman, is the zero option an option?

Mr. LIEBERMAN. I hope not. I mean, to me, the zero option for Afghanistan is the worst option for the United States of America. It does dishonor the men and women of the American military who fought there, were wounded there, and died there. It also creates all the danger for the United States that General Keane has talked about.

We have got to have some patience here. I know we set the deadline for making a decision on this is December 2014. But as General Keane has said, there is going to be an election coming up. President Karzai has taken this position. Incidentally, let's not forget that just a short while ago he summoned a loya jirga, one of the sort of people's meetings, leaders from around the country on this subject. What did they do? They voted to urge him to quickly enter into a security or status of forces agreement, bilateral, with the United States of America. The Afghan people know the terrible fate that awaits them if we pull out.

It will be terrible for us, not only in terms of it becoming a sanctuary for terrorists who will strike us again, but that is a critically important part of the world geostrategically. It will be important for our security and our prosperity to have an American presence there for some time to come. So zero option for Afghanistan is the worst option for America.

Chairman MCCAUL. Excellent point.

Ms. Harman.

Ms. HARMAN. We can't leave a force there without a status of forces agreement. That would compromise their security. I think the SOFA will be signed this year, either by Karzai or his successor, and I think the administration will decide to leave a force of some size, small force there.

But that doesn't fix the problem of Afghanistan. The government of Afghanistan has to show more responsibility for the whole country. The government of Pakistan, some impressive early start by Nawaz Sharif, has to show responsibility there, close neighbor of Afghanistan, for doing more to quell the existence of terror cells, terror organizations inside of Pakistan. Similarly in Iraq. Maliki has to govern all of Iraq. Other governments in the Middle East also have to step up.

So my bottom line is we do have a responsibility to project our values and be helpful in the Middle East. I don't think we should retreat. I do think our narrative is not where it needs to be. We also have a responsibility to use all of our Government power, soft, smart, and hard, against terror cells there which might have the capability to attack our interests or attack our homeland.

This committee has done a good job of staying focused on it. I am very pleased you asked me to participate on the panel. I would just urge one more time that on a bipartisan basis you attack these problems and show the rest of the House that bipartisanship can thrive, especially when the critical interests of the United States are at stake.

Chairman MCCAUL. We thank you for being here today as well.

Dr. Jones.

Mr. JONES. I was recently in Afghanistan, so my views are formed at least in part by that recent visit and my service there and my time since 2001 there.

I think an exit, the zero option would be extremely dangerous for the United States. In my most recent trip I visited several of the countries in the region. Their leadership, from India, from Russia, even from Pakistan itself, and from several of the Central Asian governments, the assessments from those countries is dire if there was an American withdrawal from Afghanistan. So that view is shared by all of Afghanistan's neighbors. I think the kinds of discussions we have had here about a lighter footprint, training, I think are exactly what we are talking about and exactly what we need for Afghanistan.

I would just say I have been somewhat impressed by at least some of the Afghan security services' ability to keep key provinces like Kandahar. It is the center of gravity for the Taliban, it is where their inner shura was, that is largely in the control, at least much of it is, by Afghan and allied forces. So there has been some positive developments.

This is more than just about security. I think, as Congresswoman Harman, said this is an Afghan government responsibility. But we cannot leave. We did that once. We left the region after the Soviet withdrawal and we paid a major price for that.

Chairman MCCAUL. Well, thank you, Dr. Jones.

Let me just end by saying that I do believe we need a counterterrorism footprint there after we withdraw in 2014. General Keane, perhaps you are correct, we need to wait until the next election to achieve that.

But I do believe—and, Jane, as you have mentioned—this is a bipartisan, I think most people on both sides of the aisle agree with your assessment on this issue. I know the administration is working hard towards that end.

So let me just close by saying thank you to all of the witnesses. This has been very insightful and a very distinguished panel. As you know, there will be additional questions in writing from Members. I ask that you respond to those. The record will be held open for 10 days.

And, without objection, the committee stands adjourned.

[Whereupon, at 12:49 p.m., the committee was adjourned.]

APPENDIX

QUESTIONS FROM HONORABLE PAUL C. BROUN FOR HONORABLE JOSEPH I.
LIEBERMAN

Question 1. The first step of addressing any problem is to honestly identify it, yet this administration repeatedly refuses to acknowledge the nature of our threat overseas and at home. From Benghazi to Falluja, the administration seems more focused on protecting their political message than confronting the threats still posed by radical Islamic groups operating under the ideology of al-Qaeda. Do you view this forced ignorance as a major threat to our security? Do you see any way the Obama administration will pivot towards a more honest foreign policy?

Answer. Response was not received at the time of publication.

Question 2. Our National defense is one of the few areas the Federal Government SHOULD be spending money on according to the Constitution, yet many in the administration would like to preserve other, questionable spending in favor of cutting our defense. With the Asia Pivot and growing threats in the Middle East, is that position by the administration irresponsible?

Answer. Response was not received at the time of publication.

QUESTIONS FROM HONORABLE RICHARD HUDSON FOR HONORABLE JOSEPH I.
LIEBERMAN

Question 1a. My subcommittee oversees the Transportation Security Administration, so I know all too well, from Classified meetings and briefings, just how real the threats are to our transportation systems. TSA Administrator John Pistole has stated publicly that terrorists are developing more sophisticated ways of smuggling explosives onto U.S.-bound aircraft from overseas through advanced designs and concealment methods. In 2012, we thwarted an attack by AQAP so to me it's clear the terrorists are making progress. The question I think we need to ask ourselves is—are we one step ahead or one step behind?

Answer. Response was not received at the time of publication.

Question 1b. In your assessment, are our homeland security efforts adequately adapting resources, technology, and manpower to counter the ever-changing threats to transportation security?

Answer. Response was not received at the time of publication.

Question 1c. Does the Obama administration's narrative help or hurt in this regard?

Answer. Response was not received at the time of publication.

Question 1d. What suggestions do you have that will help us stay flexible and adaptive in our approach to protecting our aviation systems?

Answer. Response was not received at the time of publication.

Question 2. How would you describe the command and control from al-Qaeda in Pakistan, led by Zawahiri, over al-Qaeda ideologically-aligned groups such as AQAP, ISIL, al-Shabaab, Ansar al Sharia, etc. Specifically how are we adapting our procedures, intelligence-gathering methods, and resources to ensure we're infiltrating and collecting accurate information on these smaller, decentralized, localized groups?

Answer. Response was not received at the time of publication.

Question 3. What impact to our homeland do you see from a complete withdrawal from Afghanistan?

Answer. Response was not received at the time of publication.

Question 4. Prior to the September 11, 2012 attack on our consulate in Benghazi, there was a great deal of reporting that al-Qaeda ideologically-aligned groups were operating in and around Benghazi. Why do you think that administration did not see those groups as a significant threat to United States operations in the area?

Answer. Response was not received at the time of publication.

QUESTIONS FROM HONORABLE PAUL C. BROUN FOR HONORABLE JANE HARMAN

Question 1. The first step of addressing any problem is to honestly identify it, yet this administration repeatedly refuses to acknowledge the nature of our threat overseas and at home. From Benghazi to Falluja, the administration seems more focused on protecting their political message than confronting the threats still posed by radical Islamic groups operating under the ideology of al-Qaeda. Do you view this forced ignorance as a major threat to our security? Do you see any way the Obama administration will pivot towards a more honest foreign policy?

Answer. Response was not received at the time of publication.

Question 2. Our National defense is one of the few areas the Federal Government SHOULD be spending money on according to the Constitution, yet many in the administration would like to preserve other, questionable spending in favor of cutting our defense. With the Asia Pivot and growing threats in the Middle East, is that position by the administration irresponsible?

Answer. Response was not received at the time of publication.

QUESTIONS FROM HONORABLE RICHARD HUDSON FOR HONORABLE JANE HARMAN

Question 1a. My subcommittee oversees the Transportation Security Administration, so I know all too well, from Classified meetings and briefings, just how real the threats are to our transportation systems. TSA Administrator John Pistole has stated publicly that terrorists are developing more sophisticated ways of smuggling explosives onto U.S.-bound aircraft from overseas through advanced designs and concealment methods. In 2012, we thwarted an attack by AQAP so to me it's clear the terrorists are making progress. The question I think we need to ask ourselves is—are we one step ahead or one step behind?

In your assessment, are our homeland security efforts adequately adapting resources, technology, and manpower to counter the ever-changing threats to transportation security?

Answer. Response was not received at the time of publication.

Question 1b. Does the Obama administration's narrative help or hurt in this regard?

Answer. Response was not received at the time of publication.

Question 1c. What suggestions do you have that will help us stay flexible and adaptive in our approach to protecting our aviation systems?

Answer. Response was not received at the time of publication.

Question 2. How would you describe the command and control from al-Qaeda in Pakistan, led by Zawahiri, over al-Qaeda ideologically-aligned groups such as AQAP, ISIL, al-Shabaab, Ansar al Sharia, etc. Specifically how are we adapting our procedures, intelligence-gathering methods, and resources to ensure we're infiltrating and collecting accurate information on these smaller, decentralized, localized groups?

Answer. Response was not received at the time of publication.

Question 3. What impact to our homeland do you see from a complete withdrawal from Afghanistan?

Answer. Response was not received at the time of publication.

Question 4. Prior to the September 11, 2012 attack on our consulate in Benghazi, there was a great deal of reporting that al-Qaeda ideologically-aligned groups were operating in and around Benghazi. Why do you think that administration did not see those groups as a significant threat to United States operations in the area?

Answer. Response was not received at the time of publication.

QUESTIONS FROM HONORABLE PAUL C. BROUN FOR JOHN M. KEANE

Question 1. The first step of addressing any problem is to honestly identify it, yet this administration repeatedly refuses to acknowledge the nature of our threat overseas and at home. From Benghazi to Falluja, the administration seems more focused on protecting their political message than confronting the threats still posed by radical Islamic groups operating under the ideology of al-Qaeda. Do you view this forced ignorance as a major threat to our security? Do you see any way the Obama administration will pivot towards a more honest foreign policy?

Answer. Response was not received at the time of publication.

Question 2. Our National defense is one of the few areas the Federal Government SHOULD be spending money on according to the Constitution, yet many in the administration would like to preserve other, questionable spending in favor of cutting our defense. With the Asia Pivot and growing threats in the Middle East, is that position by the administration irresponsible?

Answer. Response was not received at the time of publication.

QUESTIONS FROM HONORABLE RICHARD HUDSON FOR JOHN M. KEANE

Question 1a. My subcommittee oversees the Transportation Security Administration, so I know all too well, from Classified meetings and briefings, just how real the threats are to our transportation systems. TSA Administrator John Pistole has stated publicly that terrorists are developing more sophisticated ways of smuggling explosives onto U.S.-bound aircraft from overseas through advanced designs and concealment methods. In 2012, we thwarted an attack by AQAP so to me it's clear the terrorists are making progress. The question I think we need to ask ourselves is—are we one step ahead or one step behind?

Answer. Response was not received at the time of publication.

Question 1b. In your assessment, are our homeland security efforts adequately adapting resources, technology, and manpower to counter the ever-changing threats to transportation security?

Answer. Response was not received at the time of publication.

Question 1c. Does the Obama administration's narrative help or hurt in this regard?

Answer. Response was not received at the time of publication.

Question 1d. What suggestions do you have that will help us stay flexible and adaptive in our approach to protecting our aviation systems?

Answer. Response was not received at the time of publication.

Question 2. How would you describe the command and control from al-Qaeda in Pakistan, led by Zawahiri, over al-Qaeda ideologically-aligned groups such as AQAP, ISIL, al-Shabaab, Ansar al Sharia, etc. Specifically how are we adapting our procedures, intelligence-gathering methods, and resources to ensure we're infiltrating and collecting accurate information on these smaller, decentralized, localized groups?

Answer. Response was not received at the time of publication.

Question 3. What impact to our homeland do you see from a complete withdrawal from Afghanistan?

Answer. Response was not received at the time of publication.

Question 4. Prior to the September 11, 2012 attack on our consulate in Benghazi, there was a great deal of reporting that al-Qaeda ideologically-aligned groups were operating in and around Benghazi. Why do you think that administration did not see those groups as a significant threat to United States operations in the area?

Answer. Response was not received at the time of publication.

QUESTIONS FROM HONORABLE PAUL C. BROUN FOR SETH G. JONES

Question 1. The first step of addressing any problem is to honestly identify it, yet this administration repeatedly refuses to acknowledge the nature of our threat overseas and at home. From Benghazi to Falluja, the administration seems more focused on protecting their political message than confronting the threats still posed by radical Islamic groups operating under the ideology of al-Qaeda. Do you view this forced ignorance as a major threat to our security? Do you see any way the Obama administration will pivot towards a more honest foreign policy?

Answer. My current research and past counterterrorism experience in the U.S. Department of Defense indicates that the threat from al-Qaeda and other Salafi-jihadist groups remains significant. The number of Salafi-jihadist groups, fighters, and attacks has increased since 2010. Most of the attacks are occurring in North Africa and the Middle East in such countries as Yemen, Somalia, Iraq, and Syria. Indeed, the war in Syria has been the single most important attraction for Salafi-jihadist fighters. This increase in Salafi-jihadist groups has likely been caused by weakening governments across North Africa and the Middle East, as well as the expansion of Salafi-jihadist operatives that have spent time at terrorist training camps, fought on jihadist battlefields, or been released or escaped from prison.

The threat posed by this diverse set of Salafi-jihadist groups varies widely. Some are locally-focused and have shown little interest in attacking Western targets. Others, like al-Qaeda in the Arabian Peninsula, present a substantial threat to the U.S. homeland, along with inspired individuals like the Tsarnaev brothers that perpetrated the April 2013 Boston Marathon bombings. In addition, several Salafi-jihadist groups pose a medium-level threat because of their desire and ability to target U.S. citizens and structures overseas, including U.S. embassies. Examples include Ansar al-Sharia Tunisia, al-Shabaab, the Muhammad Jamal Network, al-Qaeda in the Islamic Maghreb, and the various Ansar al-Sharia groups in Libya. As explained below in response to the second question, there are significant risks in downplaying the threat from al-Qaeda and other groups plotting attacks against the U.S. homeland and U.S. interests abroad (such as embassies).

Question 2. Our National defense is one of the few areas the Federal Government SHOULD be spending money on according to the Constitution, yet many in the administration would like to preserve other, questionable spending in favor of cutting our defense. With the Asia Pivot and growing threats in the Middle East, is that position by the administration irresponsible?

Answer. It is vital that the United States retains a defense budget capable of defeating and deterring terrorist groups plotting attacks against the U.S. homeland and U.S. interests overseas. The trends noted above suggest that the United States needs to remain focused on countering the proliferation of Salafi-jihadist groups, despite the temptation to shift attention and resources to the Asia-Pacific region and to significantly decrease counterterrorism budgets in an era of fiscal constraint. The U.S. Department of Defense's 2014 Quadrennial Defense Review, for example, notes that the United States should be "principally focused on preparing for the future by rebalancing our defense efforts in a period of increasing fiscal constraint." It also emphasizes the importance of the Asia-Pacific region as "increasingly central to global commerce, politics and security."[1] Not surprisingly, much of the U.S. military—including the Army, Air Force, Navy, and Marine Corps—is shifting its attention to the Asia-Pacific theater, including such issues as force posture, acquisitions, campaign planning, and response anti-access area-denial (A2AD) challenges.

This rebalance entails risks, particularly if it involves decreasing attention and resources from countering the resurgence of al-Qaeda and other Salafi-jihadists in North Africa and the Middle East. For the near future, some of the most acute security threats to the U.S. homeland and its interests overseas will come from terrorist groups and state sponsors of terror in North Africa and the Middle East, not countries in the Asia-Pacific. To complicate matters, most U.S. Government agencies involved in counterterrorism have not systematically apportioned or adequately synchronized their declining resources to focus on the most serious terrorism threats.

With the U.S. shift to Asia, it is important that the United States continue to provide sufficient resources and attention to North Africa and the Middle East for the use of special operations, intelligence, diplomatic, and other capabilities to conduct precision targeting of groups and their financial, logistical, and political support networks. The United States also needs to continue training, advising, and assisting local governments in their struggle against terrorism. For the foreseeable future, the United States will need to orchestrate covert raids to capture or kill terrorists, seize their supplies, and target their finances; conduct air strikes from drones, fixed-wing aircraft, and helicopters; oversee psychological operations to undermine terrorist support; collect and analyze intelligence about terrorist groups (their networks, locations, capabilities, and intentions); and engage with Tribal and other local actors.

QUESTIONS FROM HONORABLE RICHARD HUDSON FOR SETH G. JONES

Question 1a. My subcommittee oversees the Transportation Security Administration, so I know all too well, from Classified meetings and briefings, just how real the threats are to our transportation systems. TSA Administrator John Pistole has stated publicly that terrorists are developing more sophisticated ways of smuggling explosives onto U.S.-bound aircraft from overseas through advanced designs and concealment methods. In 2012, we thwarted an attack by AQAP so to me it's clear the terrorists are making progress. The question I think we need to ask ourselves is—are we one step ahead or one step behind?

Answer. Whether we are one step ahead or one step behind depends, in part, on the issue. According to several documents found in Osama bin Laden's Abbotabad residence, some senior al-Qaeda leaders were frustrated about the difficulties in smuggling operatives into the United States because of improvements in U.S. border security, intelligence collection and analysis, and databases such as the No-Fly List. However, terrorists—including al-Qaeda and its affiliates—continue to innovate. In Somalia, al-Shabaab has explored the possibility of concealing bombs inside consumer electronic items, such as laptop computers, cameras, and tape recorders. And al-Qaeda in the Arabian Peninsula bomb makers continue their efforts to build improvised explosive devices using components that may not be detected by airport screeners.

Perhaps most concerning, al-Qaeda is a different organization than it was a decade ago—a development that some officials have not fully appreciated. The broader Salafi-jihadist movement has become more decentralized among four tiers: (1) Core al-Qaeda in Pakistan, led by Ayman al-Zawahiri; (2) formal affiliates that have sworn allegiance (or bayat) to core al-Qaeda (located in Syria, Somalia, Yemen, and North Africa); (3) a panoply of Salafi-jihadist groups that have not sworn allegiance to al-Qaeda but are committed to establishing an extremist Islamic emirate; and (4)

---

[1] U.S. Department of Defense, *Quadrennial Defense Review 2014* (Washington, DC: U.S. Department of Defense, 2014), pp. IV, 4.

inspired individuals and networks. Using the state of core al-Qaeda in Pakistan as a gauge of the group's strengths (or weaknesses)—as some have done—is increasingly anachronistic. Overall, I am concerned that the United States is one step behind in understanding the nature of the threat from a heterogeneous and decentralized movement.

Question 1b. In your assessment, are our homeland security efforts adequately adapting resources, technology, and manpower to counter the ever-changing threats to transportation security?

Answer. I have not done a thorough analysis of whether—and how much—U.S. homeland security efforts are adequately adapting resources, technology, and manpower to counter the evolving threats to transportation security. However, other RAND researchers have examined various aspects of transportation security.[2] One of the biggest gaps in U.S. homeland security efforts is the absence of a veritable counterterrorism strategy. A strategy refers to a plan to defeat or degrade terrorist groups. Government officials need to consider how to use their military, law enforcement, diplomatic, financial, and other tools against terrorist groups. The British government, for example, has a comprehensive counterterrorism strategy referred to as CONTEST, which covers transportation and other types of security. It is based on four areas of work: Pursue (to stop terrorist attacks); prevent (to stop people becoming terrorists or supporting terrorism); protect (to strengthen our protection against a terrorist attack); and prepare (to mitigate the impact of a terrorist attack). While the United States does have a National Strategy for Counterterrorism in name, it does not offer a veritable plan for how to combine resources, technology, manpower, and other key ingredients to defeat terrorist groups.[3] This is a notable gap in countering the ever-changing threats to transportation and other types of security.

Question 1c. Does the Obama administration's narrative help or hurt in this regard?

Answer. My current research and past counterterrorism experience in the U.S. Department of Defense indicates that the threat from al-Qaeda and other Salafi-jihadist groups remains significant. According to my analysis, the number of Salafi-jihadist groups, fighters, and attacks has increased since 2010. Approximately 98 percent of the attacks are occurring against local targets, particularly in North Africa and the Middle East. Examples include groups operating in Tunisia, Algeria, Mali, Libya, Egypt (including the Sinai), Lebanon, and Syria. In fact, the war in Syria has been the single most important attraction for Salafi-jihadist fighters.

More broadly, the United States lacks a coherent narrative to combat the narrative of al-Qaeda and other Salafi-jihadists. In 1999, the State Department disbanded the U.S. Information Agency, which played a prominent role in countering Soviet ideology during the Cold War. Today, no U.S. Government agency has the lead role for countering the ideology of al-Qaeda and its broader movement. The State Department has the lead for public diplomacy, including through such organizations as the Center for Strategic Counterterrorism Communications. But the State Department has not developed—nor has the mandate for—a comprehensive interagency strategy to counter al-Qaeda's ideology. The CIA is involved in some clandestine activity, but most senior officials do not view undermining al-Qaeda's ideology as its core mission. The Department of Defense is also involved in some efforts, but they are dispersed among U.S. Central Command, U.S. Special Operations Command, and other organizations. Ultimately, it is the President and the National Security Staff's responsibility to appoint a lead agency and hold it responsible. An effective campaign has to be done carefully, covertly, and led by credible Muslims in these countries. In the end, the struggle against the al-Qaeda movement will be long—measured in decades, not months or years. Much like the Cold War, it is also predominantly an ideological struggle.

Question 1d. What suggestions do you have that will help us stay flexible and adaptive in our approach to protecting our aviation systems?

Answer. The recent tragedy with Malaysia Airlines flight MH370 highlights the need to improve passport security, with two passengers that boarded the flight using stolen passports. Both of the stolen passports had been on Interpol's Stolen

---

[2] See, for example, Andrew R. Morral, et al., *Modeling Terrorism Risk to the Air Transportation System: An Independent Assessment of TSA's Risk Management Analysis Tool and Associated Methods* (Santa Monica, CA: RAND, 2012); Brian Michael Jenkins, *Aviation Security: After Four Decades, It's Time for a Fundamental Review* (Santa Monica, CA: RAND, 2012); Kevin Jack Riley, *Air Travel Since 9/11* (Santa Monica, CA: RAND, 011); Brian A. Jackson, *Efficient Aviation Security: Strengthening the Analytic Foundation for Making Air Transportation Security Decisions* (Santa Monica, CA: RAND, 2012).

[3] White House, *National Strategy for Counterterrorism* (Washington, DC: White House, June 2011).

and Lost Travel Documents (SLTD) database, but the airport and airline staff failed to make the necessary checks. This is a gaping loophole for terrorist organizations and poses a threat to Americans traveling overseas. Interpol created its Stolen and Lost Travel Documents database in 2002, and it now contains more than 40 million records. The SLTD database is available to Interpol's 190 member states, but only a few countries systematically search the database—such as the United States, United Kingdom, and United Arab Emirates. According to Interpol, passengers were able to board planes more than a billion times in 2013 without having had their passports screened.[4] Additional measures are being made to enhance passport security such as the installation of chip and fingerprints in the documents, but it is still a vulnerable system. The United States should take the lead in encouraging and assisting other governments in fixing these loopholes.

In addition, one of the most important steps to protecting U.S. aviation systems is to ensure U.S. intelligence agencies are providing U.S. Government agencies dedicated to protecting U.S. aviation systems with sufficient information about the types of plots and improvised explosive devices being developed—or considered—by terrorist groups.

Question 2. How would you describe the command and control from al-Qaeda in Pakistan, led by Zawahiri, over al-Qaeda ideologically-aligned groups such as AQAP, ISIL, al-Shabaab, Ansar al Sharia, etc.? Specifically how are we adapting our procedures, intelligence-gathering methods, and resources to ensure we're infiltrating and collecting accurate information on these smaller, decentralized, localized groups?

Answer. Al-Qaeda's command and control is increasingly decentralized. Core al-Qaeda includes the organization's leaders, most of which are based in Pakistan. Al-Qaeda's senior leadership retains some oversight of the affiliates and, when necessary, may attempt to adjudicate disputes among affiliates or provide strategic guidance. But Zawahiri's failure to mediate the dispute between Jabhat al-Nusrah and the Islamic State of Iraq and al-Sham highlights core al-Qaeda's limitations.[5] However, the U.S. Government needs to better adapt its procedures, intelligence-gathering methods, and resources to an expanding number of Salafi-jihadist groups. Most U.S. Government agencies involved in counterterrorism have not systematically apportioned or adequately synchronized their declining resources to focus on the most serious terrorism threats.

Question 3. What impact to our homeland do you see from a complete withdrawal from Afghanistan?

Answer. A complete U.S. withdrawal from Afghanistan could seriously jeopardize U.S. security interests because of the continuing presence of al-Qaeda and other terrorist groups in Afghanistan and Pakistan. U.S. forces would have little or no mandate and limited or no capabilities after 2015 to assist the Afghan government if the Taliban or other groups associated with al-Qaeda threatened to overrun a major city or even topple the government. A U.S. withdrawal would also increase the probability that Afghanistan would be used as a beachhead for al-Qaeda and other militant groups. Iraq after the U.S. withdrawal is illustrative: al-Qaeda in Iraq has regrouped since 2011. It conducts attacks at a high tempo and was instrumental in establishing an affiliate, Jabhat al-Nusrah, in Syria.

A civil war or successful Taliban-led insurgency would likely allow al-Qaeda and other terrorist groups such as the Tehreek-e-Taliban Pakistan, Haqqani network, and Lashkar-e-Taiba to increase their presence in Afghanistan. Most of these groups have already expanded their presence in Afghanistan over the past several years and have conducted attacks either against the U.S. homeland (al-Qaeda and Tehreek-e-Taliban Pakistan), U.S. forces and U.S. Government installations in Afghanistan (Taliban and Haqqani network), or U.S. citizens in the region (Lashkar-e-Taiba and al-Qaeda).

In addition, al-Qaeda and associated movements would likely view the withdrawal of U.S. military forces from Afghanistan as their most important victory since the departure of Soviet forces from Afghanistan in 1989.

Question 4. Prior to the September 11, 2012 attack on our consulate in Benghazi, there was a great deal of reporting that al-Qaeda ideologically-aligned groups were operating in and around Benghazi. Why do you think that administration did not see those groups as a significant threat to United States operations in the area?

Answer. Prior to the September 2012 attack in Benghazi, U.S. Government agencies had warned of terrorist activity in the area, including from groups like Ansar

[4] Mike Hills, "Mystery of Flight MH370 Raises Fears of Passport Fraud," *BBC*, March 11, 2014.

[5] See, for example, Qaedat al-Jihad Organization—General Command, "Statement Regarding the Relationship of the Group of Qaedat al-Jihad with the Group of the Islamic State in Iraq and al-Sham," various jihadist forums, February 2014.

al-Sharia Libya, al-Qaeda in the Islamic Maghreb, and the Muhammad Jamal Network. Going forward, as some RAND work has concluded, the security plan for the U.S. diplomatic presence abroad must include well-developed strategies to both detect and prevent an assault like the one in Libya before it occurs.[8] Technology, for example, can help. Cameras with pattern-recognition software positioned around the embassy to monitor the streets can show what those streets look like on a normal day and what they look like on a day when there may be protests or an attack. They can capture protesters mobilizing or attackers prepositioning themselves before an assault. Similarly, predictive analytics can be applied to social media collected from Facebook, Twitter, and other accounts to determine when crowds might form or when an attack is being planned.

○

---

[6] William Young, *Embassy Security: From the Outside In* (Santa Monica, CA: RAND, 2013).